Study Guide to

Turtles All The Way Down

by John Green

by Ray Moore

"The Hindu Earth." Author unknown. Published in *Popular Science Monthly*, Volume 10, 1876. The image is in the public domain. (Source: Wikimedia Commons.)

Acknowledgements

As always, I am indebted to the work of numerous bloggers, reviewers and critics. Where I am conscious of having taken an idea or a phrase from a particular author, I have cited the source in the text. Any failure to do so is an omission which I will immediately correct if it is drawn to my attention. I believe that all quotations used fall under the definition of 'fair use.'

Thanks are due to my wife, Barbara, for reading the manuscript, for offering valuable suggestions, and for putting the text into the correct formats for publication. Any errors which remain are my own

Preface

A Study Guide is an aid to the close reading of a text; it is never a substitute for reading the text. This novel deserves to be read reflectively, and the aim of this guide is to facilitate such a reading. The study guide questions have no answers provided. This is a deliberate choice. I am writing for readers who want to come to their own conclusions about the text and not simply to be told what to think about it by someone else. Even 'suggested' answers would limit the exploration of the text by readers themselves which is my primary aim.

In the classroom, I found that students frequently came up with answers that I had not even considered, and, not infrequently, that they expressed their ideas better than I could have done. The point of this guide is to open up the text, not to close it down by providing 'ready-made answers.' Teachers do not need their own set of predetermined answers in order effectively to evaluate the responses of their students.

The commentaries do not set out to answer the questions, although sometimes they do cover the same ground. Each commentary represents my best understanding of a chapter at this point in time. They make no claim to be definitive. Feel free to disagree.

The questions (without the notes and commentaries) are also provided in a separate section for ease of use in the classroom or in reading groups.

Body Outlines

The male and female body outlines are from ClipArtBest.com. They are free for commercial use.

Spoiler alert!

If you are reading the book for the first time, you may wish to go straight to the "Study Guide: Notes, Questions and Commentary" or the "Study Guide: Questions" sections and come back to the introductory materials later since they do take a view of the whole text.

Contents

Turtles All the Way Down by John Green

Teacher's Introduction

Plot Summary

Aza Holmes, a 16-year-old student at White River High School, Indianapolis, battles obsessive compulsive disorder (OCD). At lunch in the school cafeteria, her best friend Daisy tells her that local billionaire construction magnate Russell Pickett has disappeared just before the police were going to arrest him and that there is a $100,000 reward for information leading to his capture. Aza is so consumed by an anxiety thought spiral that she pays little attention, though she remembers the missing man's son, Davis Pickett whom she met when she was eleven at a summer camp for kids with a dead parent, which they called Sad Camp.

After school, Daisy impulsively directs Aza to drive toward the Pickett house to check a motion-sensitive camera that Aza has remembered. The two take Aza's canoe across the White River and sneak into the Pickett compound where Aza finds the camera and downloads a photograph of the escaping Russell Pickett just before they are caught by the security guard who takes them to see Davis. It is clear that Davis and Aza still have feelings for each other. This only encourages Daisy to gather evidence (including the police report) on Russell's disappearance, while Aza looks into Davis's use of social media over the past few years. She comes to the conclusion (as she tells Daisy) that "'he seems … sweet, I guess'" (60) which, as Daisy points out, is not really much help in locating his father.

Daisy arranges a double date for herself and Mychal and Aza and Davis. It is clear than Davis is attracted to Aza, but he worries that she is only dating him because she wants the reward, so he gives Aza $100,000 and she promises not to turn the photograph over to the police. For a while, both Aza and Daisy put the mystery disappearance to one side to concentrate on their dating. However, Aza becomes increasingly aware of the unhappiness about his father's unexplained disappearance of Davis's younger brother, Noah.

Aza's OCD prevents her from having a normal dating relationship with Davis because whenever they touch or kiss her microbial anxieties kick in. She finds numerous blog posts written by him after his father's disappearance in which he also describes his relationship with her in a very positive way. In contrast, Aza also reads Daisy's *Star Wars* fan fiction for the first time and discovers herself portrayed in the frustrating, impossible character of Ayala. She comes to realize how difficult it must be for Daisy to be her friend. In terms of the disappearance of Russell,

Daisy is no longer interested since she has got her share of the money from Davis; Aza feels like she wants to discover the truth for Noah's sake, but admits that she has nothing to go on.

The suppressed tensions in Aza's friendship with Daisy come to the surface, culminating in a heated argument while Aza is driving which results in a car accident. Aza spends several weeks recuperating in the hospital and at home during which time the two rebuild their friendship.

Mykal's work is included in an underground art exhibition held inside an unfinished drainage tunnel system off Pogue's Run, an underground stream. Aza and Daisy go exploring on their own, and Aza finally solves the mystery of where Russell Pickett went and what happened to him. Aza tells Davis that the body of his father is probably in the tunnel, and subsequently he makes an anonymous tip to the police, who find the body.

Davis and Noah decide to relocate to Colorado, where Noah will attend a school for troubled youths. Aza shares the main details of her life as an adult, wife and mother coping, and failing to cope, with her psychological problems, but surviving.

Why Read this Book?

If S. E. Hinton (*The Outsiders*, etc.), Paul Zindel (*The Pigman*, etc.), Lois Duncan (*I Know What You Did Last Summer*, etc.), Judy Blume (*Forever*, etc.) and Robert Cormier (*The Chocolate War*, etc.) virtually invented the Young Adult novel, writers like Laurie Halse Anderson (*Speak, Twisted, Wintergirls, Catalyst*) and John Green (*Looking for Alaska*, *Paper Towns*, *The Fault in Our Stars*) continue to take it to a new level.

John Green certainly has a massive following, and many consider this to be his best novel to date. As of Nov. 2017, the novel gets 4.5/5 stars on amazon.com, 4.8/5 on barnesandnoble.com, and 4.2/5 on goodreads.com.

Important: Issues with this Book

The language is realistic 'teen-speak' and some readers could find the swear words and sexual references offensive. However, there is no actual sex in the book. A more significant issue is that, although the novel is very funny in parts, it is also rather dark when it comes to questions about the meaning of life and fear of the inevitability of death. Some readers might even have to think about such things for themselves!

A Note on Graphics

1. The cover illustration: "The Hindu Earth" shows the turtle standing on solid ground, but what is that solid ground? Notice that it simply appears to exist in a vacuum. Once we ask, what is the ground on which the turtle

stands, we have to admit, as the Hindu sage originally did, that we have no conception. That being so, the idea that the turtle stands on another turtle and that from there it's turtles all the way down is not a bad answer. It is an answer that says, "There is no final cause, get used to it." The ground in the illustration is rather like the Big Bang. "It all started with the Big Bang," we say, until someone asks, "And what started the Big Bang?" Perhaps we reply, "God," only to get the question, "And what brought God into being?"

2. Plot graph: Allows students to take notes on the main phases of the narrative.

3. Human outlines: These can be used for a variety of note-making activities by students. Titles might include:

How Aza sees herself;
How others see Aza;
How I [the student] see myself;
How others see me.

Dramatis Personæ – List of Characters

Characters marked * are mentioned in the narrative but play no (or virtually no) part in the action.

Aza Holmes, the novel's protagonist, struggles with obsessive-compulsive disorder (OCD), mostly stemming from a fear of the human microbiome (the human body, specifically her human body, being inhabited by millions of microbial cells, some malignant). She is constantly paranoid about infection, particularly the life-threatening bacteria called *Clostridium difficile.* One symptom of her OCD is that she obsessively reopens, drains and medicates a never-fully-healed callous on her finger in an effort to kill what she believes are pathogens. Aza is introverted, neurotic, and constantly the victim of invasive thoughts (intrusives) that take control of her consciousness. Thus, Aza's OCD, or what she describes as the devil inside her that prompts the intrusive thoughts that overwhelm her, is the real antagonist in the novel. Green describes Aza thus, "She is trying to be a good daughter, a good friend, a good student, and maybe even a good detective, while also living within the ever-tightening spiral of her own thoughts" (quoted by Drexel). The choice of family name is obviously an homage to that greatest of detectives Sherlock Holmes.

Ms. Holmes is a ninth-grade math teacher at the same high school Aza attends. She is a widow, her husband having died suddenly of a heart attack despite her own efforts to revive him. Very conscious of Aza's psychological problems, she worries a great deal about her daughter. However, she feels largely helpless to stop Aza's pain.

Daisy Ramirez, whom Aza says has played the role of "my Best and Most Fearless Friend" for years (2), is self-confident, assertive and protective of Aza who writes that "Daisy's self-proclaimed life motto was 'Break Hearts, Not Promises. She kept threatening to get it tattooed on her ankle when she turned eighteen" (6). Aza says that Daisy "lacked the capacity to experience embarrassment" which she means as a compliment (30). It is Daisy who talks Aza into going to the Pickett estate to try to get a lead on the missing businessman, and thus be able to claim the reward money.

Elena* is Daisy's eight-year-old sister with whom she shares and room, and whom she (reluctantly) has to babysit on occasions.

Mychal Turner is Aza's only other close friend whom she says plays the role of "The Artsy One" (2). He is an aspiring artist. He and Daisy have an on-and-off dating relationship.

Russell Davis Pickett Sr. is the billionaire CEO of Pickett Engineering, "an Indianapolis-based … construction firm employing more than ten thousand people worldwide" (15). He disappears from his luxury home on September 8th, the night before police planned to arrest him following "a fraud and bribery investigation" (15). A reward of $100,000 is offered for information leading to his arrest.

Russell Davis Pickett Jr. (Davis) is Russell's son. Aza remembers their time together at a summer camp when she was eleven. They "never talked much, or even looked at each other, but it didn't matter, because we were looking at the same sky together." She adds, "It's quite rare to find someone who sees the same world you see" (9). Given Aza's very personal anxieties and phobias, this is really quite a statement; it indicates that the two had once been very close. When they meet up again as a result of Daisy's investigation, they find that they still have feelings for each other. Davis is incredible understanding and supportive of Aza.

Noah Pickett is Davis's thirteen-year-old brother. He is very into space combat video games particularly after his father disappears when he becomes very introverted. Davis tells Aza, "*if Dad gets caught because he tries to contact us, that will be okay. But if he gets caught despite NOT reaching out to us, Noah will be crushed, He still thinks our dad loves us and all that*" (81).

Simon Morris is Russell's lawyer.

Detective Dwight Allen* is in charge of the hunt for Russell.

Lyle is the only security guard at the Pickett compound. He finds Aza and Daisy on the grounds and takes them to Davis to whom he seems to be very loyal.

Malik Moore is the resident zoologist on the Pickett estate. He mainly looks after the tuatara (a type of lizard).

Rosa is the house manager (housekeeper and cook) at the Pickett house. She is devoted to Davis and Noah.

Sandra Oliveros* is the senior reporter on the *Indianapolis Star* story about Russell Pickett's disappearance. Daisy spoofs her email to trick her assistant, **Adam Bitterley***, into sending her the police report of the case.

Josephine Jackson* is the banker at Second Indianapolis Bank whom Simon Morris gets to take care of depositing the $100,000 for Aza and Daisy.

Narrative Voice

Turtles All the Way Down is narrated in the first person by the protagonist, Aza Holmes. The narrative is retrospective, which means that from the very start the narrator knows how things worked out (or failed to work out). Aza makes this clear on the very first page when she writes, “If these forces had given me a different lunch period, or if the tablemates … had chosen a different topic of conversation, I would have met a different end – or at least a different middle.” The reader can infer from this that the events that will be narrated had a significant effect on the person who narrates them.

Two questions must necessarily be asked of any first person narrative. First: Does the reader trust that the narrator gives an accurate account of what happens and a reliable interpretation and evaluation of its significance? Second: Is the reader convinced that the author intends the reader to trust the narrator? Everything is fine provided that the answers to these questions are either both in the affirmative or both in the negative because each of these implies that the text has consistency and artistic integrity. Problems occur when one of the answers is affirmative and the other negative because this implies a loss of artistic control by the author and a flawed work of art. Fortunately, in the case of *Turtles*, it is perfectly clear that Aza is an unreliable narrator and that Green knows her to be so.

Grady gives the following account of Green’s use of first-person narrative in the novel:

> Aza’s obsessive inner monologue is the meat of *Turtles All the Way Down*. The story is told in a tight first-person perspective – or it is until Aza’s intrusive thoughts become so overwhelming that she splits into other perspectives – so that the reader is always trapped inside Aza’s head, where she’s unable to redirect her thoughts away from the same destructive cycle. When she’s kissing the quirky-John-Green-hero boy she likes, she’s obsessed with the idea that the microbes on his tongue are infecting her body. When she’s trying to hang out with her best friend, she keeps getting distracted by the idea that she needs to clean the cut on

her hand again.

As perceptive and accurate as that is, it is also a little complex, so let's try to unpack it. Aza sees the world, from which she often feels distant, and her physical and psychological *self*, from which she often feels alienated and whose reality she sometimes questions, through the filter of her OCD. She does not describe things as they are but as she perceives them to be. Other characters in the novel often see the world and Aza's *self* very differently. The perceptive reader sees both versions and knows their relationship.

Setting

Exactly when this story is set, we are never told. The narrative opens in September and ends just after Christmas vacation, but the year is never stated. We do know that Aza drives a sixteen-year-old Toyota Corolla, a model introduced in 1966. That would mark the earliest year for the story as 1982. On the other hand, the Corolla is still being produced, and The Lower Pogue's Run Tunnel Project (the contract for which went to Parsons Brinckerhoff not to Pickett Engineering) was not completed until 2015. There are few other details that establish the date of the story, but the references to computer technology and the Internet would suggest a year in the twenty-first century a year or two either side of 2010.

Right at the end of the narrative, the reader learns that Aza has written the story (perhaps as part of her on-going treatment for OCD) as an adult. It was clear from the first sentence that the narrative was retrospective, but it comes as a shock to learn that the narrator has grown up, had children, loved them, got "too sick to care for them," been hospitalized, got better, got sick again, and carried on with life (285). This would make the narrator middle aged which would date the narrative to the late 2020s or 2030s.

Structure

The narrative is chronological. It tells the story of five months in the life of sixteen-year-old Aza Holmes – or rather it tells two stories: the story of the psychological crisis through which Aza struggled during those months and the story of her external life as a high school student and amateur sleuth. Of these two, interconnected, plots, reviewers are united in concluding that the former is by far the more important. Thus, Maeve15 writes:

> The most important storyline of the book, however, is Aza's relationship with her own mind. She wages a constant battle with obsessive compulsive disorder, or OCD, an anxiety disorder characterized by intrusive and repeated thoughts. This creates a unique, compelling narrative that makes *Turtles All the Way Down* John Green's best book yet.

The article "Micro Review: *Turtles All the Way Down*" (which has no named author) makes much the same point:

> [S]olving the mystery of disappearance is merely a side plot. The book is essentially about Aza navigating through all the usual teenage experiences: self-discovery, first love, managing friendships, and dealing with parents. *Turtles All the Way Down* offers us a unique perspective as the protagonist's point of view is quite different and detailed. Aza suffers from an anxiety disorder for which she is being treated. She is constantly worried about how exposure to germs affects her personal microbiome. You follow her spirals of thought without getting impatient with her as her thoughts take interesting tangents.

The two extracts above present (it must be admitted) the consensus view about the novel. However, one can agree with the analysis of the relative importance of the two plots without necessarily agreeing with the evaluation of the success of the novel.

Readers should at least consider the possibility that the plot and sub-plot are *not* sufficiently connected. Indeed, for large portions of the middle portion of the novel the investigation-plot virtually disappears, and both Aza's failure to crack the case and her eventual breakthrough appear unconnected to her OCD. A reader should also ask whether the main plot really does have enough progression or whether (like one of Aza's thought spirals) it centers around itself in a series of repetitions that do ultimately become rather predictable and annoying. [Note: I do not say that this perspective is the 'right' one. I simply say that readers should consider it.]

The final two sections of the last chapter unexpectedly leap forward at least a full decade and possible two. They establish that, for Aza and Davis, there was no fairytale ending. They did not live 'happily ever after,' but they did live out their separate lives. Solving the mystery of Russell Pickett's disappearance did not cure Aza; Davis could not be the answer to Aza's psychological problems. Green is to be commended for avoiding the conventional happy ending.

Themes

> Green's works often are concerned with the idea of finding truth, even when that truth may come with doubt. (*Kenyon News*)

Obsessive-Compulsive Disorder (OCD)

In 2015, John Green wrote, "I've known that I have this mental illness for a long time, and I've had a lot of therapy and learned a lot of strategies for dealing with my illness" (Redddit). In another place, he added, "This is my first attempt to write directly about the kind of mental illness that has affected my life since childhood, so while the story is fictional, it is also quite personal" (Penguin UK). Aza Holmes is, as she tells us repeatedly, mostly a pretty ordinary (read "normal-ish") high school student, "I went to class, got good grades, wrote papers, talked to Mom after lunch, ate dinner, watched television, read … I was not *only* crazy" (93). The problem is, however, that though intrusive thoughts may leave her for hours or days, they always come back dragging her away from the real world until she is trapped in "thought spirals" and exists only in her own head. Thus, Aza will describe an ordinary situation in which she is involved, like a double date or watching a movie or kissing a boy whom she really likes, but her description will be cut off by anxieties about contracting an infection like *Clostridium difficile*, or feeling that, deep down, there is no reality to her identity. As a result, Aza is unable to function in the world around her because of her obsessive thoughts.

Turtles All the Way Down uncompromisingly depicts how Aza's relationships are affected by her OCD. Her only real friend, Daisy, gets annoyed with her; her mother constantly asks how she is feeling, but feels helpless to take away her pain; Davis, her perhaps boyfriend, does everything he can to accept her issues. Even her therapist, Dr. Singh, does not really understand how OCD makes Aza feel. How could she because the language does not exist to describe it? During the course of the narrative, the reader sees Aza's condition deteriorate rather than improve. We see her desperate attempts to combat her anxieties with rational thought continually fail. For example, after kissing Davis, she is so terrified of having his microbes in her body that her mind forces her to drink from a bottle of hand sanitizer that she always carries for the cut on her finger. (It does not seem to occur to her that hand sanitizer contains as much as sixty-two percent ethyl alcohol and may cause alcohol poisoning and even death.) Hargrove concludes, "Rationally, she knows how dangerous this is, but she can't help herself. She is a prisoner to her own compulsions. This book focuses on creating an experience for readers to truly understand what it's like living with OCD."

Grady comments that the authenticity of the novel's presentation of OCD comes from Green's personal experience:

> After the runaway success of *The Fault in Our Stars* and the movie it became, he found it so hard to write a follow-up that he went off his medication and fell into an anxiety spiral. (Worry not for the impressionable youths; one of the things Aza learns over the course of *Turtles All the Way Down* is that taking your medication can help you.) So Aza's story accordingly feels real, and exhausting, and authentic.

One could certainly manufacture a list of other themes in the book (parenting, dating, corruption in business, friendship, etc.), but they are really side-issues.

Figurative Language and Symbols

Green makes the following general point about the use of imagery and symbolism in literature:

> The great thing about figurative language and symbols and the like in novels is that you don't have to be conscious of them for them to work. (Penguin UK)

He is undoubtedly correct. For the majority of readers, images and symbols in a text work subliminally (i.e., they are perceived and reacted to intuitively without the reader being conscious of them). Of course, some readers do become conscious of images and symbols particularly when they recur or form a pattern in a text, and this consciousness can add significantly to a reader's enjoyment and appreciation of a text. Literary critics, on the other hand, frequently analyze these recurrences and patterns to evaluate their contribution to the meaning and impact of a text.

What Green's comment does not mention, however, is the possibility that the images and symbols in a text are used so insistently, so crudely, that readers are made conscious of them whether they will or no. In such a case, this consciousness can detract significantly from a reader's enjoyment, understanding, and appreciation of a text. Haig criticizes Green's use of "figurative language and symbols" in this novel on precisely these grounds:

> Some of the recurring mental illness metaphors couldn't have been hammered harder by Thor himself; it feels as though the illness-as-spiral idea occurs at least once a chapter, and there are more stargazy sentimental Big Moments than at a Coldplay concert.

With these comments in mind, readers need to address two related questions: 1. What are the important images and symbols? and 2. How effective are they in contributing to the impact and meaning of the text?

"Turtles all the way down"

> Big fleas have little fleas,
> Upon their backs to bite 'em,
> And little fleas have lesser fleas,
> and so, *ad infinitum* [i.e., and so on forever].
> (Traditional Nursery Rhyme)

Turtles All the Way Down by John Green

In a 1599 letter written from Chandagiri, India, the Jesuit Priest Emanual de Veiga (1549-1605) reported the belief of a Hindu guru that "the earth [is] supported by seven elephants, and the elephants do not sink down because their feet are fixed on a tortoise. When asked who would fix the body of the tortoise, so that it would not collapse, he said that he did not know." This belief was reported by various Western authors during the next three centuries (Samuel Purchas in *Purchas His Pilgrims*, 1613/1626; John Locke in *An Essay Concerning Human Understanding*, 1689; Henry David Thoreau in his journal, 4 May 1852). However, in 1794, Johann Gottlieb Fichte pointed out that if there is no answer to the question, "On what does the turtle stand?" then there can be no "firm foundation" upon which to base human knowledge because there is no "system of human knowledge dependent upon an absolute first principle" (*Concerning the Conception of the Science of Knowledge Generally*; A. E. Kroeger, Trans.).

A partial answer to the dilemma appears in 1836 in a (presumably) comic dialogue between an old woman and a schoolboy printed in the article "Unwritten Philosophy" in the *New York Mirror*. The boy, looking to show off his knowledge, informs the woman that the world "is not exactly round, but resembles in shape a flattened orange; and it turns on its axis once in twenty-four hours." She replies that she knows that the world "don't turn round, for if it did we'd be all tumbled off; and as to its being round, any one can see it's a square piece of ground, standing on a rock!" When challenged to say on what the rock stands, she replies, "Lud! child, how stupid you are! There's rocks all the way down!" By 1854, the phrase appears in its modern form – turtles having replaced rocks. Apocryphal versions of the above story are told involving, among others, the American psychologist and philosopher William James (1842–1910), and the British philosopher Bertrand Russell (1872–1970) who challenge an old woman in their audience who has stated that the earth rested on the back of a turtle, only to be bested by the reply, "It's turtles all the way down." The phrase had become part of the language. Daisy tells Aza a version of this story on pages 244-245. [Most of the information in the two paragraphs above is adapted from the Wikipedia article on the phrase "Turtles All the Way Down," see Bibliography.]

The answer "there are tortoises/turtles all the way down" is, however, unsatisfactory: it is merely an example of the problem of infinite regress in epistemology (the theory of knowledge). Unless there is a necessary foundation to knowledge then, as Thoreau writes in his journal, "No man stands on truth." Joel Richeimer, Professor of Philosophy at Kenyon College, writes, "All knowledge has to have a foundation. Something has to be at the bottom. So if you believe in modern physics, you say what's at the bottom is atoms. That explains everything. Or if you're a religious person, you might say it's God" (*Kenyon News*).

Other Images

Dr. Singh tells Aza, "'You often try to understand your experience through metaphor Aza … One of the challenges with pain – physical or psychic – is that you can really only approach it through metaphor. It can't be represented the way a table or a body can. In some ways pain is the opposite of language'" (88-89). [Readers can easily confirm the validity of this statement. Try to describe a really excruciating headache or toothache. In all probability, your first two words will be, "It's like…," and what will follow will be an image.]

Thus, the book is full of images that Aza uses to describe how she feels. The image of the spiral or gyre into which she is sucked recurs frequently, but others crop up as they come into her head. It is like: being a character in a play whose lines and movements are determined by someone else; not being the driver of the bus of one's own consciousness; being the canvas on which someone paints and not the artist who paints; etc. Most of these images are identified in the chapter commentaries and/or the questions.

Turtles All the Way Down by John Green

Study Guide: Notes, Questions and Commentary

The Questions are designed to focus your first reading of the text (though they will, of course, still be useful if you happen to have read the book already). The aim is to help you to understand the text, not to test you. They do not normally have simple answers, nor is there always one answer. Consider a range of possible interpretations – preferably by discussing the questions with others. Disagreement is encouraged! For the reasons stated above, no answers are provided. The Commentaries do not set out directly to answer the questions, though they may cover some of the same ground. They make no claim to be either definitive or complete.

ONE

Notes:

The notes on this chapter clarify Aza's references to her health. I have kept them brief.

"bacteria" (3) – single-cell microorganisms living in soil, water, organic matter, the bodies of plants and animals, including humans – may be beneficial or dangerous to the host.

"*digestive tract*" (3) – the route food passes through the body: mouth, pharynx, esophagus, stomach, small intestine, and large intestine.

"parasitic organisms" (3) – a parasite lives on, and at the expense of the host (fleas or lice living on humans, for example).

"microbial" (3) – an effect (disease would be a negative example) caused by bacteria.

"biome" (3) – a community of plants and animals that occupies a distinct region (such as the human body).

"*Clostridium difficile*" or "*C. diff.*" (4) – a kind of bacteria that "exists all around us. It's in the air, water, soil, and in the feces of humans and animals" – can cause a potentially fatal infection (Web MD).

"Cleveland Clinic" (5) – a very highly regarded non-profit academic medical center in Ohio.

Questions:

1. Describe a time when you felt that your life was being directed by what Aza calls, "forces so much larger than myself than I couldn't even begin to identify them" (1). How did you get into that situation? How did you feel about it at the time? How did you get out of it?

2. Explain what Aza means when she says that she "realized I might be

fictional" (1). She gives three images to describe what she means. The first is that she is a character in a story. What are the other two?

3. Aza says that she is "a skin-encased bacterial colony." Explain what she means. She also says that she "would argue that it isn't irrational to be concerned about the fact" (3). Is she right about that in your opinion?

4. What does Aza mean when she describes herself as being in a "'Thought spiral'" (8)?

Commentary:

Notice the way in which the school is described so that it sounds impersonal and unattractive. The phrase "publically funded institution" (1) makes it sound like a prison or an asylum. The "fluorescent cylinders spewing aggressively artificial light" (2) make those inside seem like victims. Probably every reader of this novel will identify with Aza's feeling that she is not in charge/ control of her own life (or, to put the same thing into the language of literary criticism, that she lacks 'agency'). What teenager has not railed against the rules, regulations and schedules of their high school? Nevertheless, Aza feels this much more intensely than most teens because of her "anxiety problems" (3). What Aza is unable to feel is any solid sense of *who she is as a person*; she fears that she may be "fictional" – a creation of "forces so much larger than myself than I [she] couldn't even begin to identify them" (1). She defines herself in terms of her relation to others: a character in a story, not the author; a canvas, not the painter; a stereotyped character in a play, not the playwright; the "Sidekick," not the epic hero; Ms. Holmes Daughter, not a named character. Aza feels that she exists only as a result of the actions of others upon her. Even the story she is about to tell happened because of the decisions and actions of others.

The other way in which Aza's identity anxiety is unique to her is that while she acknowledges that all of the students in the cafeteria "were basically identical organisms" (2), she alone is alienated from her physical body. The idea that her body is the biome to billions of microbes (some her own and some parasitical; some benevolent and some malignant) concerns her – to say the least. She says, "if half the cells inside you are not you, doesn't that change the whole notion of me as a singular pronoun, let alone as the author of my fate?" (5). Aza lives in almost constant fear that "there was something wrong with the microbial balance of power inside [her]" (4). This hypochondria is another aspect of Aza's fear that she is not in control of her own fate. She obsessively re-reads articles on bacteria and the symptoms of illness. No wonder Aza feels that thoughts like this take her down a "recursive wormhole" (5), or thought spiral that "never actually ends. It just keeps tightening, infinitely" (7) – a clear reference to the title of the novel.

All of Aza's anxieties lead to the callous on the end of her middle finger which she feels compelled to open up to let out any infection that might already be present. This is a form of self-harming (cutting) – a desperate attempt to purify herself. The reader is not surprised to learn that Aza is having psychological counseling, nor that it does not appear to be working! The reader *is* surprised to learn, right at the end of the chapter, that in Davis Pickett she once found "someone who sees the same world you see" (9). Technically, this device is called a hook, that is, a detail that catches or keeps the reader's interest.

Aza's connection with the real world is tenuous. She hardly listens to the conversation around the lunch table because the sound is drowned out by her obsessive thoughts and "*the* [supposed] *cacophony of* [her] *digestive tract*" (3). As a result, she makes very little contribution to the discussion, about which she is aware enough to feel rather guilty.

There is another level of irony in Aza's concern that she is "fictional" (1) because, of course, *she is*: Aza is a character in a novel by John Green and she has no reality except in the mind of her creator, the author, and of her re-creator, the reader.

Daisy Ramirez is an excellent foil for Aza. [The Wikipedia article on "Foil" defines it as "a character who contrasts with another character (usually the protagonist) in order to highlight particular qualities of the other character."] Daisy comes across as someone with a very firm sense of who she is. As a result, she is assertive (as when she improves on Mychal's photo-project idea), self-assured (as when she says of herself, speaking in the third person, """Daisy Ramirez won't break her promises, but she will break your heart""" [6]), and able to stand up against a bully (as when she flinches for only "a second, then straightened her spine" and delivers a brilliant repose to the girl who mocks her """Kool-Aid dye job""" on her hair [8]). She must also be patient and supportive because being Aza's friend cannot be easy.

The best comment on the opening chapter I have found is this:

> The book begins with all the banal tropes and trappings of teen fiction. A 16-year-old main character, narrating in the first person; an overly cheerful and blithe best friend who

serves as comic relief; a love interest; and the sudden disappearance of a wanted criminal with a price on his head, whose escape vexes the police, and our young protagonists are the only ones with any kind of lead.

It's a paint-by-numbers beginning so cliché that most literary agents would reach for the trash bin after the first few pages, but in typical John Green fashion, the oh-dear-not-another-one-of-these opening act is a clever setup to deconstruct common young-adult literary plots and tropes, and rebuild them into something fresh and unique. (Menard)

TWO

Notes:

"'Human Microbiota'" (10) – this Wikipedia article about the totality of microorganisms that reside on or within the human body is there for you to read.
"Paul's First Letter to the Corinthians" (13) – "Charity suffereth long, and is kind; charity envieth not; charity vaunteth not itself, is not puffed up" (13:4 *King James Version*).
"norovirus" (18) – a very contagious virus that can be passed on from close contact with an infected person, contaminated food or water, or by touching contaminated surface.
"Skee-Ball" (16) – an arcade game played by rolling balls up an inclined lane (like a miniature bowling lane) to score points when they fall into holes of descending size and ascending points value.

Questions:

5. What do you find significant about Aza's relationship with her mother?

6. What do you find significant about Aza's relationship with her car (Harry)?

7. Why do you think that Aza goes along so readily with Daisy's plan to go to the Pickett house?

Commentary:

Ms. Holmes is a teacher and in Aza's high school! Understandably, Ms. Holmes is concerned about her daughter's mental state and is constantly seeking reassurance that Aza is "'okay'" – which must be pretty annoying for Aza (10). Nor is Aza entirely honest with her mother because she lies about taking her meds daily. The truth is, "I took it, on average, maybe thrice weekly" (11). This is an important point about Aza to bear in mind: because she has no confidence in her medication, she is simply not taking it as prescribed. Nevertheless, the two seem to have a good relationship. Her mother understands Aza's feelings of being controlled and the two are able to joke about it.

How much does Green intend us to psychoanalyze Aza to find the source of her phobias and anxieties? It is, of course, impossible to know, but it is also irresistible. The death of her father when she was eight has obviously had a profound effect on Aza (even if it has not 'caused' her anxieties, it has certainly made them worse). It explains her "real love" for Harry (13) since, "Harold had been my dad's car – in fact, Dad had named him Harold" (14). The car seems to be a father-substitute. Ironically, although it is Harry's dependability that Aza loves, "in the end, Harold's imperfect audio system happened to be the last note in the melody of coincidences that changed my life" (14). Once again she stresses that she was not the author of her own destiny; however, that musical metaphor rather suggests that, looking back, Aza is glad that it did.

It is obvious why Daisy immediately decides that they are going to check out the Pickett home. She is the adventurous one, the risk-taker, and she is the one who has decided that "'there's a hundred grand waiting for is'" if they can only find Russell Pickett. Why the naturally anxious Aza should join in the adventure is less clear. However, note that she tells us "without Daisy even telling me to, I got in the right lane to drive … [t]oward Davis's house" – she calls it Davis's house, not the Pickett house or Russell's house (18). We have already learned that at summer camp she had crush on him. However, Aza explains that her house and the Pickett house are on opposite sides of the river: "Mom and I lived on the side that sometimes flooded. The Picketts lived on the side with the stone-gabled walls that forced the rising waters in our direction" (15). This seems to be a variation on the old saying about people living on opposite sides of the (railroad) tracks: it implies a huge social and financial gulf between the two families. Aza recalls "playdates at a mansion that contains a golf course, a pool with an island, and five waterslides" (16).

There seems to be another reason: Aza gets pulled into solving the puzzle of Russell's disappearance. She really seems to enjoy working out the possibilities that, given Russell's escape route, he tripped the camera that she remembers. At least solving this mystery takes her mind off of the microbial battle being waged in her own body for a while.

THREE

Notes:

"pterodactyl" (24) – extinct flying reptile of the late Jurassic period.

Questions:

8. How does Daisy feel about her Chuck E. Cheese uniform? Are her feelings the same as Aza's feelings at the start of Chapter One, or are they different?

9. There is a rather long (overly long?) retrospective of one of Aza's childhood birthdays on Pirates Island. What is the point of this recollection?

10. Aza describes the sight of the sky through the branches of a dead tree which "intersected to fracture the cloudless blue sky into all kinds of irregular polygons" (24). What reflection does that sight cause Aza to have?

Commentary:

Clothes are important in this chapter. Daisy wants to change out of her Chuck E. Cheese uniform before meeting a billionaire. She complains that uniforms are designed "so that you become, like, a nonperson, so that you're not Daisy Ramirez, a Human Being … It's like the uniform is designed to *hide me.*" Daisy also notices that Ms. Holmes appears to wear a uniform that serves the same function because, as she tells Aza, "'Your mom dresses like a ninth-grade math teacher'" (20). Both women have their individuality stolen by a uniform, or rather by the vast anonymous entities that employ them. This strikes the reader as both true and similar to Aza's thoughts at the start of the novel. The difference is that Daisy analyzes the issue rationally, which gives her some measure of control (agency); in contrast, Aza allows herself to become overwhelmed by the thought of the loss of her identity.

When Aza recalls the time in her childhood when she and Daisy played in the canoe up and down the White River, it is clear that this was before her phobias and anxieties really took hold. When Daisy threw a daddy longlegs at her, Aza would "scream and run away, flailing my arms but not actually scared, because back then all emotions felt like play like I was experimenting with feeling…" This leads Aza to a profound truth. She tells us, "True terror isn't being scared; it's not having a choice in the matter" (22). She remembers the innocence of her childhood adventures with Daisy, Davis and Noah on Pirates Island and says nostalgically, "I was so good at being a kid, and so terrible at being whatever I was now" (25).

Aza's eleventh birthday party on Pirate Island was one such perfect moment of childhood and both she and Daisy remember it as such. Aza, however, also remembers that Davis "really freaked out" when he thought he had lost his Iron Man action figure, which functions like a security blanket – a clear sign of his having suffered from psychological issues even then (26).

Two things about Aza in this chapter strike both her and the reader as out of character. First, having gone into great detail about how polluted the White River is, when it comes to wading from Pirates Island to the Pickett compound, she and Daisy "waded through the knee-deep water until we got to the river's edge." Even in retrospect, Aza cannot answer her own question, "Why didn't it bother me to slosh through the filthy water of the White River when hours earlier I'd found it intolerable to hear my stomach rumble? I wish I knew" (26). The reader might answer that in solving the mystery Aza is directing her attention outward (the very opposite of a thought spiral) and that she has just remembered a time in her childhood when the water held no microbial terrors for her. Second, not only does Aza take the initiative in getting through the chain-link fence, but she is "the calm one while feeling Daisy's nerves jangling" when, as someone approaches them. Again, Aza states the purely personal nature of her anxieties, "the things that make other people nervous have never scared me. I'm not afraid of men in golf carts or horror movies or roller coasters. I didn't know precisely what I was afraid of, but it wasn't this" (27). This again reminds the reader of Aza's helplessness in the face of her anxieties: they control her.

Aza's description of the sky seen through the branches of a dead tree which "intersected to fracture the cloudless blue sky into all kinds of irregular polygons" is followed by the memory that her father took "[a] ton of pictures … of leafless branches dividing up the sky." She comments, "I always wondered what he saw in that, in the split-apart sky" (24). This is the second reference Aza has made to staring up into the sky (the first being Davis and her "staring up at a cloudless summer sky … looking at the same sky together" [9]), so the reader might anticipate more such descriptions. Haig comments critically that in the novel "there are more stargazy sentimental Big Moments than at a Coldplay concert." Apart from the rather obvious conclusion that in such moments Aza manages to feel an intimate contact with someone else who sees the same world that she does (which, given her anxieties, hardly ever happens), it is premature to interpret this motif.

It is only a small detail, so a first-time reader might miss it, but what Russell was wearing in the photograph is important. It is a huge clue to the nature of his disappearance and to his eventual fate. That said, it is not one that either Daisy or Aza seems to pick up on.

FOUR

Notes:

"geodesic dome" (30) – round dome constructed of rigid triangles and glass.
"a tuatara" (35) – reptile resembling a lizard – native to New Zeeland.
"reticulated" (35) – built out of net (in this case, chrome).
"Picasso" (37) – Pablo Picasso (1881-1973) – Spanish artist best known for his paintings though he worked in a wide variety of forms – perhaps the greatest of the modernists, his works sell for millions of dollars.
"Rauschenberg" (37) – Milton Ernest 'Robert' Rauschenberg (1925-2008) – innovative pop culture American artist.

Questions:

11. When Davis offers Aza a Dr. Pepper, she tells us she was "a little confused" (31). Explain why.

12. What is "the truth" that Aza is tempted to tell Davis at the end of the chapter?

Commentary:

The reader can see from Aza's reaction to the Pickett estate that she finds it easier to relate to inanimate things than she does to people. She comments, "The Pickett estate was silent, sterile, and endless – like a newly built housing subdivision before actual people move into it. I loved it" (29). The word "sterile" points to Aza's dilemma because it means both "free from bacteria or other living microorganisms; totally clean," and "unproductive infertile unfruitful … barren … lacking in imagination, creativity, or excitement; uninspiring or unproductive" (Oxford dictionaries). Aza's problem is that real life comes with bacteria.

Aza is surprised that Davis remembers her – so well, in fact, that he remembers that her favorite soda is Dr. Pepper. Aza is momentarily "a little confused" by this presumably because, as we have seen, her own memories of Davis are also clear (31).

The issue of personal identity is raised again. Davis laments that his father gave him his own full name (Russell Davis Pickett) making the son indistinguishable from the father. When Aza reassures him that he is not his name, Davis replies, "'Of course I am. I can't not be Davis Pickett. Can't not be my father's son … And I can't not be an orphan'" (33). Davis feels that he has no identity other than that which has been imposed on him. This is reflected also in the people who work on the estate: Lyle tells

Daisy "'I *am* security here'" (30); Malik is introduced by Davis as "'our zoologist'" (35); and Rosa is "dressed all in white," a uniform that indicates her position as house manager. When Aza sees her, she comments, "I looked at her and thought about Daisy's observation about uniforms" (37).

In contrast to this is Aza's name, given to her by her father because, as he explained to her, "It spans the whole alphabet, because we wanted you to know you can be anything" (33). Ironically, these good intentions have not materialized since Aza is perhaps the most inhibited of the characters, prevented from being herself by her phobias and anxieties. In fact, she even doubts that she has an independent identity.

Aza is pretty inarticulate when she says goodbye to Davis because she has feelings for him that she finds it hard to acknowledge. She wants to tell him why she needs the callous on her finger, which would involve telling him about her fear of infection, but she cannot bring herself to do so.

[Am I the only reader who finds the last two chapters more than a little slow?]

FIVE

Notes:

"seropurulent drainage" (47) – all wounds drain as a natural stage in the healing process, but drainage of yellow pus is often a sign of infection.
"Centers for Disease Control" (47) – the leading national public health institute of the United States.

Questions:

13. Explain what "intrusives" are (45). If everyone has them, what makes Aza's intrusives so different from those most people have?

Commentary:

Aza gives five reasons why dating seems to her to be impossible: two have to do with the exchange of bodily fluids (saliva and sweat) which means opening her body to invasive bacteria, and three have to do with her inability to keep her thoughts on the date and therefore her inability to say the right things at the right times.

OK, Russell Pickett leaving his billions to his tuatara (or more accurately to fund scientific research into his tuatara through which """"humans will learn the key to longevity and better understand the evolution of life on earth"""" [43]) is pretty weird. To be honest, it is the sort of thing that comes up a lot in Young Adult fiction in which the inexplicable weirdness of adults is a recurring theme. However, in this case, the detail of Russell's will actually provides a revenge motive for Davis to join Aza and Daisy in the search for his father.

Aza describes her intrusive thoughts as thoughts that "seem to arrive at my biosphere from some faraway land, and then to spread out of control." Everyone has such thoughts (they are what cause us to 'daydream'), but most people are able to dismiss them and move on with their lives. Aza, however, gets *taken over* by her "intrusives" – which is why she calls them "invasives" (45). When the idea strikes her that her finger might be infected, Aza tries to deal with it rationally, but fails; she feels compelled to reopen the wound to drain it of possible infection. What happens is that her personality literally splits and there is a dialogue between the rational half and the irrationally anxious half (represented by italic print). Notice that during Aza's account of this internal battle she refers to herself in the second person, "You're watching TV with your mom…" (45). In this way, she forces the reader to experience an invasive *as she* experiences it.

Aza's intrusives take away her free will and in doing so they take away her identity: she wants "to choose the thoughts that are called [hers]," but she cannot (46). So she opens up the callous on her finder, drains it and medicates it, but in a few hours the thought that it is infected will intrude again, "The spiral tightens, like that, forever" (47).

[Am I the only reader who thinks that you really can't have a constantly reopened cut on the end of your finger for more than five years without that cut becoming infected at some point? Would not her mother and/or her doctor have seen the constant Band-Aid as evidence of self-harming and done something about it?]

SIX

Notes:

"IRL" (54) – in real life.
"Charlotte Brontë" (56) – (1816-1855) eldest and most famous of the Brontë Sisters (the others being Emily and Anne) – the quotation is from her novel *Jane Eyre*.
"'He who doesn't fear death dies only once'" (56) – said by Giovanni Falcone (1939-1992) an Italian judge and prosecuting magistrate who waged a campaign against the Mafia and was finally assassinated – the idea is that entertaining the very thought of one's death is a kind of death: Aza's interpretation is too literal.
"Toni Morrison" (57) – (born 1931) important African-American novelist.
"DEMOCRITUS" (58) – (c. 460–c. 370 BC) Greek philosopher credited with developing the theory that matter is composed of atoms.
"William James" (58) – (1842–1910) American psychologist and philosopher who stressed the importance of evaluating ideas based on their real life consequences.
"J. D. Salinger" (59) – (1919-2010) American author whose most influential and popular novel was *The Catcher in the Rye* – the protagonist, Holden Caulfield, shouts, "Sleep tight, ya morons!" as he leaves his hated Prep School for the last time.
"ALS" (60) – "amyotrophic lateral sclerosis, is a progressive neurodegenerative disease that affects nerve cells in the brain and the spinal cord" (ALS Association).
"sensorial plane" (60) – the level of reality experienced through the five senses – the real world.
"Americans with Disabilities Act" (61) – (1990) – "a civil rights law that prohibits discrimination against individuals with disabilities in all areas of public life, including jobs, schools, transportation, and all public and private places that are open to the general public. The purpose of the law is to make sure that people with disabilities have the same rights and opportunities as everyone else" (National Network).
"skeezy" (62) – suspicious, dubious, not respectable, not to be trusted.
"megalomaniac" (62) – someone obsessed with his/her own power.
"phishing" (65) – pronounced 'fishing,' describes a range of ways a person might try to get information (data) through electronic communication by fooling the person who provides it about their identity so that they trust the source (e.g., a fake email purporting to come from a

trusted source).

Questions:

14. What more do we learn about Aza and her father?

15. What do you make of the incident with the "'dick pic'" (53)? Is this just the author playing to his Young Adult readers by being as shocking as possible without being *really* shocking? Do teenage girls really talk about stuff like this in the way Aza and Daisy do?

16. Explain what Aza means when she says, "For the record, he who does fear death also dies only once, but whatever" (56).

17. What does Aza learn about Davis from his Instagram posts and his blog (pages 56-58)?

18. How does Daisy get a copy of the police report on Russell? How does Aza react when Daisy tells her how she got it?

Commentary:

In conversation with her mother, Aza (and the reader) learns that she is very much like her late father: they are both worriers. This raises the possibility that Aza's anxiety disorder is actually genetic. Aza tells her mother, "'Worrying is the correct worldview. Life is worrisome.'" We learn that Aza's father died suddenly and that her mother still blames him. She says, "'I still can't believe he left us,'" about which Aza comments, "She said it like it was a decision, like he'd been mowing the law that day and thought, *I think I'll fall down dead now*" (52).

The conversation about the "dick pic" (56) is racy and mildly titillating, but it does not seem to have anything to do with anything else, except perhaps assuring the reader that these two teens have pretty typical teen lives outside of their very untypical situation (trying to get their hands on $100,000) and Aza's very personal anxiety neurosis. On the other hand, Green might just be playing to his teen audience.

Following Davis's social media history, Aza discovers a romance between him and a cheerleader that "seemed to have started the summer between ninth and tenth grades and lasted a few months" before ending, at least on Davis's part, since the girl still follows his posts (56). [Nothing ever seems to come of this romance which is never mentioned again.] The effect of the quotations and the reflections that follow is to convince Aza just how similar Davis's experience of the world is to her own. The Morrison quote is followed by an account of looking into the night sky, an activity he once shared with Aza; what follows the Brontë quote seems to be a recollection of him and Aza at Sad Camp; the Democritus quote is followed by an ambiguous reference to thinking "about her all the time. My stomach flips when I see her" (58) which could be about either the unnamed girl but (more likely) Aza who wrote of her reaction to seeing Davis again, "My stomach was kind of churning, but I couldn't tell why. I never understood my body – was it scared or excited?" (34); the James quote is followed by the caustic comment, "I don't know what superpower William James enjoyed, but I can no more choose my thoughts than choose my name." which is exactly the way Aza says that she experiences thoughts, "not as a choice but as a destiny. Not a catalogue of my consciousness, but a refutation of it … Davis got it. You can't choose. That's the problem" (59). (This is also an close parallel of something Aza has written earlier, "I wanted to say more but the thoughts kept coming, unbidden and unwanted. If I'd been that author, I would've stopped thinking about my microbiome…" [8].)

Daisy's success in getting a reporter to email her a copy of the police report on Russell Pickett causes Aza to panic as an intrusive thought comes unbidden and unwanted into her mind. She tries to "shake off … to swallow the thought" (64), but she cannot: What if the reporter gets fired for sending out the report? What if the 'theft' of the report is traced back to Daisy and Aza, and they are both arrested? Daisy reassures Aza that neither thing will happen and that she will protect Aza. Aza replies, "'You can't control it, that's the thing … Life is not something you wield, you know,'" but Daisy confidently replies. "'Hell yes, it is'" (66). This is the difference between the two girls (and between Aza and anyone who does not suffer from anxiety): whilst Aza tends to get sucked down a thought spiral, Daisy takes practical, effective action.

There are certain differences between Aza and Daisy. Aza reports these without appearing to be aware of their significance. For example, Daisy does not have a car. Aza writes, "Daisy didn't have a computer, so she did everything on her phone, from texting to writing fan fiction. She could type on it faster than I could on a regular keyboard" (52-53). Later, in Appleby's, Daisy has to ask for a charge from Aza's computer (61). When the check comes at Appleby's, Aza reports, "Daisy never had any money and my mom let me charge twenty-five dollars a week as long as I kept straight As" (65). Aza is so self-absorbed that she has not noticed how much more affluent she (an only child) is than her friend. This explains the very different attitudes that the two take to the prospect of getting their hands on all or some of the $100,000 reward.

SEVEN

Notes:

"to have been raptured" (76) – 'rapture' is the end-of-time event predicted in Christian theology when all believers, living and dead, will spontaneously rise into the sky to join Jesus in eternity.

Questions:

19. Ms. Holmes wants Aza to follow Dr. Singh's advice because, as she tells Aza, "'There's no need to suffer.'" Aza's unspoken response is, "I'd argue [that] is just a fundamental misunderstanding of the human predicament" (70). Explain the difference between these two approaches to the experience of being alive.

20. Exactly why does Mychal talk to Aza about asking Daisy to go out with him?

21. What pressures does Davis feel himself to be under?

Commentary:

Although there is some progress with the 'case' (i.e. finding where Russell is and getting the reward) in this chapter, that element of the plot is really progressing rather slowly since neither the police nor Daisy and Aza have much to go on. Even the police report is merely "'witness statements' from witnesses who had not witnessed anything" (74). There is the potential for conflict between Daisy and Aza, however, because Daisy is not conscious of the impact that their investigation might have on Davis and Noah. Thus, when Daisy suggests that their information about the camera might be worth something, Aza asks her not to do anything until she has talked to Davis about it because she "was worried about betraying him, even though I barely knew him" (77). Nevertheless, Daisy goes ahead and has "'a highly hypothetical conversation with the tip line.'" The distance between the understanding of the two friends is made clear when Daisy says the issue is simple, "'Crook gets caught. We get paid. I don't see why you're waffling here, Holmesy'" (78).

Aza admits that, on the one hand, she is not taking her medication "quite as often as I was technically supposed to" and, on the other hand, that she "wasn't convinced the circular pill was doing anything when I did take it." In contrast, Ms. Holmes's attitude to medication is very simple: she trusts Dr. Singh to provide the therapy that will ease, or even eliminate, her daughter's suffering. Aza's attitude is more complex. First, there is a more fundamental reason that Aza resists her medication – one that is entirely inconsistent with her earlier objection that the pills do not work. She is struck by "some way-down fear that taking a pill to become myself is wrong": this seems to her to be a paradox (i.e., a logically senseless idea). What she means is that the whole point of a drug is to change one's consciousness, but the new consciousness cannot possibly be the *real* you. Second, she rejects the idea that suffering can, or should, be eliminated from life. She writes, "I'd argue [that] is just a fundamental misunderstanding of the human predicament" (70). Possibly, on a philosophical level, Aza is more correct than her mother, but on a practical level her attitude is only going to cause her OCD to get worse.

The two witness statements of Davis and Noah are very different. To Davis there was nothing different about the day his father left. It was "just a regular day … Even looking back, there was nothing weird about that day" (74-75). Noah, however, picks out details that, at least with hindsight, suggest that his father was intending to leave: he "told Davis he needed to do a better job of watching out for me"; he "put a hand on my shoulder when he got up to leave"; and he pressed his hand on Noah's shoulder so, "It almost hurt" (75). Although he does not say so, Noah obviously believes that his father abandoned him and that is why he is do sad.

The texts that Aza exchanges with Davis show that he is having identity issues similar to hers. Just as she rejects the idea that she is the sum of the microbes inhabiting her body, so he rejects the idea that he is the sum of the vast fortune his father has built up. Davis really is "'sweet'" (60), particularly in his concern for his younger brother's welfare, but he is also out of his depth in the situation he finds himself in because this thirteen-year-old brother needs a father and Davis cannot be his father. He feels completely alone. That is why he reaches out to Aza who immediately empathizes with him: neither of them has a clear sense of their own identity and each is consumed by existential angst (put very simply, fear that life is absurd because nothing lasts). He texts, "*And the thing is, when you lose someone, you realize you'll eventually lose everyone*," and she responds "*True. And once you know that, you can never forget it*" (81). Afterwards she reflects, "[I was] thinking about his father and mine. Davis was right: Everybody disappears eventually" (82). Everyone has thoughts like this, but the difference between Aza and Davis and 'normal' people is that most people are able to put them to the back of their mind and carry on functioning. In Aza and Davis (to a lesser degree) the thoughts take over and paralyze the will.

EIGHT

Notes:

"locus" (86) – location.
"Lexapro" (88) – drug used to treat anxiety and major depressive disorder: "It works by helping to restore the balance of a certain natural substance (serotonin) in the brain … It may improve your energy level and feelings of well-being and decrease nervousness … Take this medication regularly to get the most benefit from it … Nausea, dry mouth, trouble sleeping, constipation, tiredness, drowsiness, dizziness, and increased sweating may occur … Many people using this medication do not have serious side effects" (WebMD).
"Virginia Wolf" (89) – (1882-1941) influential English writer of the modernist movement – she suffered from a manic-depressive illness and eventually committed suicide – her final note to her husband began, "Dearest, I feel certain that I am going mad again. I feel we can't go through another of those terrible times."
"connote" (89) – verb meaning a word's ability to suggest or imply a meaning beyond the literal meaning (e.g., 'red' carries connotations of danger, 'white' carries connotations of purity).
"Battle of Valhalla" (90) – refers (perhaps) to the fictional space battle (November 9th, 2401) between a hundred ships of the US and United Commonwealth fleets met and eighty-seven Imperial ships which ended the 3rd War of Barnard's Star – although there are several different versions in war games.
"gastroenterologist" (91) – specialist in the digestive system and its disorders.

Questions:

22. Do teenage girls still say "like" in almost every statement? Did they ever?

23. Dr. Singh tells Aza, "'You often try to understand your experience through metaphor Aza'" (88). Make a list of the metaphors that Aza uses to describe how she feels.

24. Comment on the repetition of the phrase "I think" at the end of the chapter (92). Is Aza right?

Commentary:

There is very little sign of plot in this chapter, except the double date that Daisy arranges between herself and Mychal and Aza and Davis. Daisy explains it all as a result of her getting "nervous on the phone" and being unsure about wanting to date Mychal, but the reader may suspect that the date is part of her cunning plan to bring Aza and Davis together in order to get the sort of information that will ultimately lead to the reward. If that is true, then we are going to have to wait a while to see how it pans out because most of the chapter is about Aza's visit to Dr. Singh and about what it feels like to be her.

Despite Aza's determination to tell Dr. Singh what she wants to hear (i.e., that her patient is getting better and putting her illness behind her), the first thing she says is, "'I feel like I might not be driving the bus of my consciousness'" (86). This is an example of what Dr. Singh calls Aza's attempt to "'understand [her] experience through metaphor … [because one] of the challenges with pain – physical or psychic – is that we can really only approach it through metaphor … In some ways, pain is the opposite of language'" (88-89).

Although Aza lies about the Band-Aid on her finger and about how regularly (or rather irregularly) she takes her meds, she asserts almost defiantly, "'I mean, I'm still crazy, if that's what you're asking. There's been no change on the being crazy front'" (86). Aza's problem is essentially that she does not know who she is: she can never "'find the deep down part … that's pure or unsullied or whatever, the part of me where my soul is supposed to be'" (87). For Aza, it is bacteria *all the way down*. She does not see pills as an answer because pills do not liberate the "'way-down you,'" they simply impose a fake identity which leads to the paranoid question, "'Who's deciding what me means – me or the employees of the factory that makes Lexapro?'" (88). There really is no answer to Aza's dilemma: she cannot find her *self* on her own, but she is convinced that drugs will not reveal her *self* – stalemate! Ironically, all of Dr. Singh's well-intentioned help only results in Aza suffering an intrusive thought: she becomes convinced that she is suffering from *C. diff* and that she is dying. Rational argument has no effect on her conviction.

Dr, Singh comes up with the profound observation that "'In some ways, pain is the opposite of language,'" and the reader is likely to be convinced. However, language is all that we have got. More importantly, it is all that a novelist has got, and here lies Green's artistic problem: he is trying to communicate *in words* how Aza feels to readers who (for the most part) have never felt the way she feels.

NINE

Notes:

"Tu-Quyen Pham" (99) – the name is quite common, but I could not locate a particular architect.
"Pettibon" (99) – (born Raymond Ginn, 1957) – Californian artist. (Search on-line images for "Pettibon spirals.")
"KERRY JAMES MARSHALL" (100) – (born 1955) – African-American painter and sculptor.
"*Tender Is the Night*" (101) – Fitzgerald's last completed novel (1934) tells the tragic story of the relationship between Dr. Dick Diver and his mentally unstable wife Nicole.
"Black Flag" (100) – originally called "Panic," an American punk rock band formed in 1976 in Hermosa Beach, California, by Greg Ginn whose brother, Raymond, did much of the artwork on their album covers.
"terrarium" (102) – sealed globe in which plants are grown.
"Cassiopeia" (103) – constellation named after Cassiopeia, the queen in Greek mythology who boasted about her unrivalled beauty.
"aneurysm" (106) – a balloon-like bulge in an artery that can prove fatal, particularly if it occurs in the brain.
"*Diplostomum pseudospathaceum*" (105) – look this up on the "Parasite of the Day" website which is a real thing that Aza would have loved!

Questions:

25. Explain how Aza uses the example of the life-cycle of the parasite *Diplostomum pseudospathaceum* to illustrate her sense of helplessness. A great way to do this would be to draw an annotated diagram of the life-cycle.

26. Explain the different attitudes of Davis and Noah to the possible return of their father.

Commentary:

As if to prove that she isn't "only crazy" (93), Aza describes the double date, including such ordinary details as putting on makeup and being warned by her mother about rich boys. [Ms. Holmes's warning to be careful of Davis because, "'Wealth is careless'" (95) seems to come right out of Scott Fitzgerald's *The Great Gatsby* where the narrator says, "'They were careless people, Tom and Daisy – they smashed up things and creatures and then retreated back into their money…'"] True, during the dates Aza does not take much part in the conversation and at one point says, "it felt like I was watching the whole thing from somewhere else, like I was watching a movie about my life instead of living it" (97), and at another, "They laughed because something was funny; I laughed because they had" (98), but this is a mild form of alienation with which most teen readers *can* probably empathize.

In the painting by Raymond Pettibon of "a colorful spiral, or maybe a multicolored rose, or a whirl pool," Aza sees the image of her thought spirals and feels herself to be drawn into the image. She writes, "It didn't feel like something I was looking at so much as something I was part of" (100).

Davis takes Aza outside and they do some more stargazing. Davis loves looking out into the universe, which is the very opposite of Aza's obsessive thoughts of herself as a biome within which she cannot locate anything that is actually *her*. For a moment, Aza shares his perspective: she lets him hold her hand and even admits that she wants to kiss him. The trouble is that Aza begins to suffer intrusive thoughts about how she is a "'mere organism'" which means that she cannot get 'into' the tender romantic moment she is having holding Davis's hand. At his prompting, Aza tries to explain. The problem that Green has is that (quite naturally) Aza *cannot* tell Davis anything more than she has already told several other people, including the reader, because Aza does not fully understand her anxieties. As she says earlier, "Even I found myself annoying" (7). So Aza feels: alienated from (or frankly grossed out by) the physical body in which she exists (in fact, in which she is trapped); insignificant against the vastness of the universe; and not in control of her own thoughts, actions and reactions; not really real, but "'just a lie I'm whispering to myself'" (105). She uses the metaphor of the life-cycle of the parasite *Diplostomum pseudospathaceum* to illustrate her sense of helplessness. This final image is new (although it is another variation on the spiral), but with this exception the reader has already heard this – several times.

Davis shares a very personal story about visiting his mother in the hospital while she was in a coma. His father kept insisting that she (that is, her *self*) was no longer real, was no longer present even though her body was physically still alive, but Davis insists that, "'She was still real. She was still alive. She was as much a person as any other person,'" and he goes on to reassure Aza that she is also "'real, but not because of your body or because of your thoughts.'" Aza's problem, we have already established, is that she cannot be sure that the things she thinks actually are *her own* thoughts. It's all very profound, but even Davis has to admit that it does not actually solve anything for Aza. She asks, "'Then what?'" and he replies, "'I don't know,'" which is a bit of an anti-climax (107).

Davis's anxiety is that he cannot believe that Aza wants to be with him for any reason other than the reward, and to be fair Aza can't actually be sure about this either. Just as Aza *cannot* forget bacterial infections, so he *cannot* forget the reward. Suddenly, Davis realizes that his problem is "'completely solvable'" (109): he simply offers Aza $100,000 *not* to turn the photograph over to the police. That way, as he tells her, "'if you still call or text or whatever, I'll know it's not about the reward. And you will too. That would be a nice thing to know – even if you don't call'" (110). Davis does not say this, but he has found a way to stop his own thought spiral from being turtles all the way down; he has found a solid certainty on which to base his relationship with Aza. [The idea that even the son of a crooked businessman guilty of bribery and corruption can just 'find' $100,000 in cash stuffed in various little hiding places strains credibility somewhat.]

Complications arise when Aza talks to Noah because the kid is in the sort of psychological mess with which she can identify. Just as much as Davis wants his father not to be found in order to protect Noah, Noah himself is desperate for his father to return. He tells Aza, "'I want him to come home … Ever since he left, I can't think straight'" (112), and Aza knows just how that feels. So Aza leaves the house with $100,000 in cash having promised Davis *not* to try to help the police find his father and with the promise that Noah will send her "'all the notes off Dad's phone from iCloud'" with the promise that she *will* look through them for clues on Russell's disappearance. This is a real-world dilemma that has nothing to do with her OCD. The detective mystery plot is heating up.

Spoiler alert: The clue to the solution to the mystery of where Russell comes on the penultimate page of this chapter (112). It will not be for about another hundred-and-fifty pages that Aza works it out!

TEN

Notes:

"'Helicopter Parenting'" (115) – increasingly a critical phrase used to describe parents who too closely monitor their children, particularly in relation to school.
"Over time, markets will always seek to become more free" (116) – a statement that sums up the philosophy of those free market economists who oppose regulation.
"Experiential value" (116) – quite simply the value that a person gains from a particular experience.
"Disgrace – Coetzee" (116) – title of a novel by South African writer, and winner of the Nobel Prize in Literature, J. M. Coetzee – it involves a man dismissed from his university post for having an affair with a female student.
"*Never Tell Our Business to Strangers: A Memoir*" (116) – by Jennifer Mascia, published 2010.
"Juan Solomon Park" (118) – on the northwest side of Indianapolis, the park (named after an African-American community leader) was originally build in the 1970 but has recently been redeveloped.
"debutant" (124) – young woman of wealthy family making her first formal appearance in fashionable society.

Questions:

27. How realistic do you find this $100,000 pay off? Come to think of it, how realistic is it that Davis and Noah would be left alone by Social Services, even though they do have lots of money?

Commentary:

There are several strands in this chapter: the clues from Russell's phone (even though they do not mean anything to Aza yet); Aza looking at the photographs on her father's phone and remembering his sudden death from a heart attack; and showing Daisy the $100,000, discussing it and spending some on a meal.

Aza's compulsion to look at her father's photographs on his phone, "which still worked eight years after his body stopped working" (117), is a way of looking back into a happier past. In this, it is the same as Davis looking into the night sky at stars whose light has taken years to reach earth: in both cases, a person is looking into the past at a time of stability – before death intervened, before the star exploded.

When Aza shows Daisy the money their different reactions are another indication of their different financial circumstances. Aza still has moral scruples: is the money "dirty"; is she "exploiting Davis" [120]; what about Noah who "'was crying and everything'" [123]? Daisy cannot afford the luxury of moral scruples. She tells Aza, "'We're not in the helping-billionaire-orphans business; we're in the getting-rich business, and business is booming.'" Their different economic perspective is also evident in Aza's comment that "'fifty thousand dollars isn't rich'" and Daisy's calculation of how long it would take her to earn that amount, and her reply that "'Maybe that's not rich to you Holmesy, but that's rich to me'" (123).

ELEVEN

Notes:

"declared an emancipated minor by the state" (126) – in *some* states a minor can be emancipated by court order – they are no longer under the care and control of parents but take responsibility for their own decisions in areas such as finance, educations, and health.
"optometrist" (129) – eye and spectacles specialist.
"sepsis" (130) – the body's overwhelming and self-destructive reaction to the infection of a wound – can lead to tissue damage, organ failure, and death.
"Edgar Allan Poe" (132) – (1809-1849) American writer famous for his macabre Gothic fiction ("The Fall of the House of Usher," "The Pit and the Pendulum," etc.) – was considered by many to have been mentally unstable.

Questions:

28. Reflecting on the (supposed) infection of her finger, Aza thinks, "*It's happening*. The *it* too terrifying and vast to name with anything but a pronoun" (132). Explain what you think she means by *it*.

Commentary:

For the first time in the novel, the reader gets to follow Aza as she is sucked into a major thought spiral. The intrusive thought that her finger is infected comes right out of the blue. In fact, as she drives Daisy to the bank, she reflects that she has felt fine all day. "I felt like a perfectly normal person," adding, "*Maybe the medicine is working*." Then the demon that forces her to think thoughts that she does *not want* to think strikes. This is how the thought spiral develops:

> *The medicine has made you complacent, and you forgot to change the Band-Aid this morning ... this is last night's Band-Aid ... the wound is open ... you left the same Band-Aid on for – God – probably thirty-seven hours ... letting it fester ...It's probably too late ... the infection is in your bloodstream ... YOU KNOW I'M RIGHT.* (128)

It is painful to watch Aza's rational mind fight a losing battle against her anxiety. Even Daisy's attempts at rational reassurance have no effect, for, as she understands, Aza's personality has split. Daisy urges her friend, "'Don't let Aza be cruel to Holmsey, okay?'" but even that has no effect (130).

Aza asks herself, "Why did I give myself a constant gaping open wound on, of all places, my finger?" (130). The reader cannot resist trying to answer that question: because you watched helplessly as your father died of a heart attack. As for the second question she implies when she says, "'I did it to myself. Like I always do'" (131) answers might include: because you are the only person who seems to be worried about Noah and you are helpless to save him; because you feel guilty about Davis giving you $100,000; because you really like Davis but can't know that you are not exploiting him; because you really like Davis but you know that you cannot have a relationship with him. These are the sort of worries that a 'normal' person might have; the difference is that with Aza they completely take over. That, of course, leads to another question: Why does Aza get sucked into thought spirals that other people can avoid? She gives the answer herself when she writes, "what I wanted to know was unknowable, because there was no way to be sure about *anything*" (130): for Aza, life is turtles all the way down.

At the bank, Aza is out of it, "the problem was I wasn't really in the bank, I was inside my head" (132); driving she "was aware of absolutely nothing outside [herself]" (133); and doing homework her "consciousness felt like a camera with a dirty lens" (134). If anything, the medication only increases this feeling. Death is the only certainty in life, but, as Aza's experience with her father taught her, "Something is going to kill you, someday, and you can't know if this is the day" (133). Life is infinite uncertainty.

TWELVE

Notes:

"Alice Walker" (138) – (born 1944) important African-American writer – author of the novel *The Color Purple* (1982).

"one of Alexander Hamilton's *Federalist* essays" (140) – the *Federalist* Papers comprise eighty-five articles and essays written by Alexander Hamilton, James Madison, and John Jay.

"Yeats's 'The Second Coming'" (144) – William Butler Yeats (1865-1939) was an Irish poet –"The Second Coming" is a complex poem that presents a nightmarish vision of the modern world falling apart.

"Robert Penn Warren" (144) – (1905-1989) – American writer – here is the full context of Davis's quotation:

> For West is where we all plan to go some day. It is where you go when the land gives out and the old-field pines encroach. It is where you go when you get the letter saying: Flee, all is discovered. It is where you go when you look down at the blade in your hand and the blood on it. It is where you go when you are told that you are a bubble on the tide of empire. It is where you go when you hear that thar's gold in them-thar hills. It is where you go to grow up with the country. It is where you go to spend your old age. Or it is just where you go.

"'Draco'" (149) – constellation of the Dragon (said to be the dragon killed by Hercules).

"gyre" (150) – a spiral, whirl or vortex – in Yeats's poem, he is concerned that the world is spinning out of control.

"campylobacter" (153) – bacterial infection that causes diarrhea (often bloody), fever, and abdominal cramp – can, in very rare cases, be life-threatening.

"cinch the lasso" (156) – secure the lasso around something, normally the pommel of a Western saddle.

"'Auld Lang Syne'" (159) – 'times long passed' – the title of a traditional Scots folk song sung to bid farewell to the old year at midnight on New Year's Eve.

"'We're here because…'" (159-160) – cynical, mocking song that British soldiers of World War I sang as they marched to the trenches where they knew that many of them would die – Why were they even there, fighting in a foreign land? No one had an answer.

Questions:

29. Daisy gets frustrated with Aza (140). Why? Is Daisy justified in feeling slightly infuriated with Aza?

30. Explain why Davis begins to cry when Ms. Holmes talks to him about Aza.

31. Look at the song Ms. Holmes sings, "'We're here because…'" (159-160). How is it related to the title and basic theme of the novel?

Commentary:

At the start of the novel Aza writes of her best friend Daisy, "Sometimes I wondered why she liked me, or at least tolerated me. Why any of them did. Even I found myself annoying" (7). The reader sees something of the strain of being Aza's friend when Daisy complains, "'I try really hard not to judge you, Holmsey, and it's slightly infuriating when you judge me'" (140). Daisy has a point, but on the other hand Aza's caution about not spending the money is actually wise, and part of Daisy's frustration probably comes from knowing this – from Aza being, on this occasion, the adult in the room. On the other hand, Daisy is right that Aza has not got a clue about what it is like never to have enough money for the things she wants.

Ms. Holmes is concerned that Davis has been brought up in a culture of entitlement because his money can buy him whatever he wants. Davis cries because no amount of money can buy him back the mother who died when he was young or the father who 'disappeared' from his life years before he physically ran off. He cries because he recognizes that Aza's mother "'gives a shit'" in a world where most adults "'"'lack all conviction'"'" (144). Ms. Holmes reminds Davis of what is missing from his life.

Davis suffers from the same anxieties about the unfathomable motives of people as does Aza. For example, Rosa has known him from childhood and says, "'you and Noah are the only little boys I have left'" (145), but she is still an employee and so lacks what Aza calls, "one of the defining features of a parent … that they don't get paid to love you" (146). Davis can never be sure that Rosa would still care for him if he were not able to pay her to do so.

Aza is able to describe to Davis the feeling of being in a "'*tightening* gyre [vortex] … that shrinks and shrinks your world until you're … stuck inside a prison cell … [and] you realize you're not actually *in* a prison cell. You *are* the prison cell'" (150). Suddenly, Aza wants Davis "badly enough that I no longer cared why I wanted him" (151-152), but after kissing him an intrusive takes her back down the infection thought spiral despite the efforts of her rational self to repel it. She feels that, as with Daisy, her anxieties have become "an irritation … to anyone who got close to me" (154), and she warns him that her condition "'doesn't get better … I'm not going to un-have this … I can't have a normal life if I can't kiss someone without freaking out'" (155). Davis is incredibly patient with her; he urges her to live in the moment and not to worry about a hypothetical future. Because she cannot conceive of a future for herself, she again takes refuge in looking at a happier past by viewing her father's photographs.

Aza sums up her total sense of alienation, "I hated my body. It disgusted me … I wanted out – out of my body, out of my thoughts, out – but I was stuck inside of this thing, just like all the bacteria colonizing me" (159). This is a powerful chapter that leaves the reader in no doubt that Aza's condition is serious.

THIRTEEN

Notes:

"Ativan" (164) – drug used to treat anxiety disorders (although it is not approved for use by anyone younger than 18) – it looks as though Aza has been told to use it occasionally as needed.
"Voldemort's name" (165) – Lord Voldemort (aka Tom Marvolo Riddle) is Harry Potter's main antagonist.
"*Ulysses* … Molly Bloom" (166) – Irish writer James Joyce (1882-1941) published *Ulysses* in 1922 – Molly is the wife of main character Leopold Bloom.
"'Descartes's philosophy'" (166) – "I think, hence I am, was so certain and of such evidence, that no ground of doubt, however extravagant, could be alleged by the sceptics capable of shaking it, I concluded that I might, without scruple, accept it as the first principle of the philosophy of which I was in search" (Rene Descartes). *Dubito, ergo cogito, ergo sum* (I doubt, therefore I think, therefore I am) was, in fact written by Antoine Léonard Thomas, though he was trying to clarify Descartes's intent.

Questions:

32. Why do you think that Aza is so fascinated by the photograph of "'that guy with the netting'" (165)?

33. How do *you* know that you exist? Have you ever doubted that you exist – that is, that there is "'a way-down deep [you] who is an actual, real person…'" (165)?

Commentary:

Finally Aza trusts Dr. Singh with her deepest fear. (She has never told her doctor what she now says but this narrative is retrospective: she *has* already shared her deepest fear with the reader in its first sentence.) She tells her, "'I think I might be a fiction'" (165) by which she means that she does not have any existence independent of outside forces (circumstances, bodily functions and malfunctions, bacteria, thoughts, etc.) over which she has no control. For once Dr. Singh does not say that this feeling is very common. Instead, she turns the idea completely around and tells Aza that her very capacity to doubt reality *proves* her own reality; it proves the existence of some deep-down entity that is *her*. This may be true, but the reader doubts that it will actually help Aza.

This is all pretty deep psychology/philosophy, and this is really not the time and place for Philosophy 101. However, it is clear that Decartes was trying to find a solid principle of certainty upon which to base human knowledge. That is, he was trying to find out what was under the last turtle, and what he found was proof of the reality of his own existence. This is precisely what Aza fails to find: Aza finds only an endless sequence of things that are *not* her but which construct her identity in ways over which she had no control.

Apart from Dr. Singh, two people are really trying to help Aza: her mother and Davis. Her mother can only help by being protective – and inevitably this sometimes means being over-protective and annoying. This is what led to her warning Davis and to her wanting to keep Aza close when she is in college. Inevitably, Aza (who is a teenager before she is a bundle of anxieties) resents this. Davis seems to be having more success. Without setting out deliberately to do it, he is showing Aza that her own perception of her body as hateful and gross are purely subjective – they are *only* thoughts. Unfortunately, it is easier for Aza to accept this idea while texting Davis than while kissing him or holding his hand.

FOURTEEN

Notes:

"centrifuge" (175) – rapidly spinning wheel used to separate the different constituents of a fluid based on their different densities.
"metabolism" (177) – the chemical processes within a living organism that maintain life.
"'*Jupiter Ascending*'" (179) – 2015 science fiction movie.
"Edna St. Vincent Millay" (180) – (1892-1950) American poet and playwright who epitomized the New Woman – in her later years, she suffered physical and psychological problems.

Questions:

34. In what ways does the plot of the novel move forward in this chapter?

Commentary:

In what way is this chapter not simply a rerun of her last kissing session with Davis – the same intrusive thought about bacterial infection; the same attempts to be rational about the risks; the same dash to the restroom? Even the explanations are hardly new, "I watched myself for a long time, trying to figure a way to shut it [the intrusive] off, trying to find my inner monologue's mute button, *trying*" (181). The metaphor *is* new, but the thought is not.

The first new element is the biology lesson Aza gets from Malik who stresses "'how *successful* [Tua] is'" (176). Tua's body actually works: for example, tuatara carry the parasite "'salmonella … but they never get sick from them'" (175). Up until this point, Aza has only thought in terms of the failure of her body to fight off malignant bacteria. Also, in Malik she discovers someone who is *not* afraid of infinite regression. His study of tuatara never provides definitive answers but, as he tells Aza, "'What I love about science is that as you learn, you don't really get answers. You just get better questions'" (177). The second new element is Noah's worsening situation. In her encounter with him, he opens up to her about missing his father. He tells her, "'It's like I can't think of anything else. I … it's …'" (181). The similarities with Aza are too obvious for her to ignore – not only the thoughts that take over Noah's being, but his inability to find words to describe them. The third new element is that, despite all of her efforts, and Davis's phenomenal patience, Aza's condition is not getting better. Their relationship seems to be moving to a crisis.

FIFTEEN

Notes:

"ROBERT FROST" (185) – (1874-1963) very popular American poet.
"infinitesimality" (185) – tiny smallness (the word does not actually exist though infinitesimal does).
"EMILY DICKENSON" (185) – (1830-1886) reclusive American poet most of whose work was only published after her death.
"JACQUELINE WOODSON" (186) – (born 1963) African-American writer of books for children and young adults.
"TERRY PRATCHETT" (186) – Sir Terence David John Pratchett, OBE (1948-2015) author of tremendously popular fantasy novels, especially the *Discworld* series.
"MAURICE SENDAK" (187) – (1928-2012) American writer and illustrator of children's books
"WILLIAM SHAKESPEARE" (187) – (1564-1616) greatest playwright and poet in any language in any age.
"Dedalus" (188) – not the figure from Greek mythology, but Stephen Dedalus the young protagonist of *Ulysses* who says, "History is a nightmare from which I am trying to awake."
"*The Tempest*" (189) – (1610-11) probably the last play Shakespeare wrote on his own – amongst other things, it is a love story.
"e. e. cummings" (189) – Edward Estlin Cummings (1894-1962) prolific American writer and artist.
"*analytics*" (190) – software that tells Davis when and for how long someone is accessing his blog.

Questions:

35. Why does Davis need Aza?

Commentary:

When she is thinking straight, Aza is a pretty good Internet detective. I'm not clear why Davis writes anonymous blogs that he does *not* want connected to him and published. He is certainly taking a risk, because if Aza can find them so could someone else, but perhaps he just needs some way of expressing his feelings about what he is going through. There is no doubt that the tone of his entries becomes more positive after Aza comes back into his life. At first she reminds him of his past and he writes, "I want the past back, no matter the cost. It doesn't matter that it won't come back, that it never even existed as I remember it – I want it back. I want things to be like they were, or like I remember them having been. Whole" (187). This is why Davis looks at stars whose images are those of years ago (because of the time light takes to travel to earth), and this is why Aza keeps looking back at her father's photographs. However, Davis moves onto a new thought. He may not be the answer to Aza's anxieties and phobias, but she certainly seems to be the answer to his, particularly because "she doesn't remind me of the past, for some reason. She feels present tense" (187-188).

The chapter ends with one of the very few positive metaphors in the novel. Describing their facetime, Aza writes, "the light that made him visible to me came mostly from a cycle: Our screens were lighting each of us with light from the other's bedroom. I could only see him because he could see me" (191). This image captures a benevolent infinite cycle. Paradoxically, however, Aza is able to feel closer to Davis during facetime than she would if they were actually face to face, "I wasn't really in my bed and he wasn't really in his. Instead, we were together in the non-sensory place, almost as if we were inside the other's consciousness, a closeness that real life with its real bodies could never match" (192). It is a touching moment, but also an ominous one if you re-read the final clause of the sentence above.

Meanwhile, what has happened to the investigative sub-plot?

SIXTEEN

Notes:

"IRL" (193) – in real life.

Questions:

36. How accurate is Daisy's depiction of Aza in the character of Ayala?

Commentary:

Apparently for the first time Aza reads Daisy's fan-fiction and finds herself portrayed as the character Ayala, the girl whom Rey (the Daisy character) calls "'my best friend and greatest burden'" (194). For the first time, Aza gets to see herself as others see her; she gets to see the impact that she has on the lives and feelings of her best friend. She writes, "I now saw myself as Daisy saw me – clueless, helpless, useless. Less." At first Aza is angry, but then she comes to the remarkably mature conclusion that "Ayala was the thing Daisy had to do to live with me" (196).

Still, things are not the same between the two girls because of the time Daisy now spends with Mychal. Even though Daisy goes out of her way to make time to be with Aza and tells her, "'I love you,'" she soon, "raced off to Mychal's place" (199). The two also have different ideas about finding Russell. For Daisy, it was all about the reward, and since they have got the money it is over; for Aza, however, it is all about wanting to help Noah. Like Ayala, Aza has, in Daisy's words, "the moral integrity of a girl who'd never been hungry" (194).

SEVENTEEN

Notes:

"Kurt Gödel" (203) – (1906-1978) "probably the most strikingly original and important logician of the twentieth century," which is strange because he was also paranoid and Aza's account of his death is accurate – although his thought is well beyond the understanding of most of us, it is linked to the infinite regression problem that is central to this novel, "Gödel's work was the surprising culmination of a long search for foundations" (United States Naval Academy) – Aza is constantly failing to find "foundations."

"interoceptive input" (209) – signals sent to the brain by the organs of the body that tell the brain how the body is functioning.

"GI tract" (209) – gastrointestinal tract – the series of organs in the human body whose function is to digest food, extract nutrients and expel waste matter.

Questions:

37. Explain the similarity that Aza finds between Davis's compulsive stargazing and her own compulsive viewing of her father's photographs.

38. How would you describe Aza's psychological state at the end of this chapter?

Commentary:

Davis explains (again) that looking at the light of a star or planet is looking at a past reality because of the time it takes light to reach the earth. Aza understands, however, that Davis's stargazing is a form of escape from present suffering. That is why she likes looking at her father's photographs: they come from a time before her present suffering. Aza concludes, "Our hearts were broken in the same places. That's something like love, but maybe not quite the thing itself" (206). This reminds the reader of Ayala's moral conscience: for Aza, the perfect is the enemy of the good – she finds compromise impossible.

At night Aza reads Davis's blog. The first entry expresses the fear that she too has, "Who knows what lies I believe, or you do? Who knows what we shouldn't doubt? …we are shipwrecked" (208). This is another way of saying that without some first cause, truth is an infinite regression so you cannot know what truth is because it's turtles all the way down. This is pretty depressing, but Davis's next post is much more positive. He notes that his time with Aza (he does not name her, of course) that evening has been like going "out to the meadow" – that is, pretty near perfect. He writes, "It was like we weren't even there, lying together by the pool. It felt like we were in some place your body can't visit…" (208). Compare this with what Aza wrote at the end on Chapter Fifteen, "I wasn't really in my bed and he wasn't really in his. Instead, we were together in the non-sensory place, almost as if we were inside the other's consciousness, a closeness that real life with its real bodies could never match" (192). They are virtually identical.

Unfortunately Aza allows herself to be drawn back into Daisy's fan fiction where she finds a version of herself that is "horrible – totally self-centered and perpetually annoying" (209). This in turn pulls her inexorably to her familiar articles on human microbial makeup, which leads to the perception that "my bacteria were affecting my thinking" (210). Her anxious self tells her "*Maybe you're not even thinking this though. Maybe you thinking's infected*" (210). The reader watches hopelessly as Aza disintegrates to the extent that she does not recognize that she *has* a *self*. For the first time, Aza actually seems self-destructive, even suicidal.

EIGHTEEN

Notes

"a CT scan" (220) – computerized tomography scan – "combines a series of X-ray images taken from different angles and uses computer processing to create cross-sectional images … A CT scan has many uses, but is particularly well-suited to quickly examine people who may have internal injuries from car accidents or other types of trauma" (Mayo Clinic).

Questions:

39. What are the criticisms that Daisy makes of Aza? Do you find them fair?

Commentary:

Plot development: Aza is driving Daisy to Appleby's, and they get into a serious car accident.

The causes of the accident are complex: Aza is over-tired and stressed. However, the immediate cause is an argument between the two that Aza starts by complaining about the character of Ayala in Daisy's fan fiction. Daisy hits back with a few home truths, telling her friend that she is "'extremely self-centered … spoiled, kinda … [and doesn't] ever think about anybody else's life'" (215-217). Part of Daisy's resentment is that Aza never seems to have realized that she does not have the material advantages that Aza takes for granted. Aza, in turn, tries to make her friend see how much worse it is for her since she is "'actually stuck inside my head with no way out'" (217). Then Aza runs into the back of the car in front.

Daisy cannot understand why Aza is so "'upset about a goddamned car … [because it's] a *car*, Holmsey. We almost *died*, and you're worried about your *car*'" (218). What she does not understand is that Aza is not crying about a car, she is crying about having totaled *her father's car* and, even more significantly, having destroyed his phone, her last point of contact with him.

The reaction of Aza's mother shows the reader that Aza is not the only one who has suffered from her father's sudden death. Ms. Holmes tells her, "'I can't lose you too'" (220). Though she does not have too, Daisy stays beside Aza, who feels, "such a failure as a daughter and a friend" (221).

Aza is concerned that she might be given antibiotics because (she believes) that will make her bacteria resistant and so make her body more vulnerable to infection.

NINETEEN

Notes:

"Sekou Sundiata" (224) – (1948-2007) African-American poet, performer and teacher.

Questions:

40. Explain fully why Aza drinks the hand sanitizer.

Commentary:

Aza has a chronic fear of hospitals based on stories of people who have picked up an infection (particularly the dreaded *C. diff.*) there and died, but her medical condition is such that she has no alternative to being admitted. She is pretty much at her lowest ebb, convinced that she "can't function in the actual sensate world … could never become a functioning grown-up … [and would always] spend a good portion of the workday terrorized by thoughts [she's] forced to think, possessed by a nameless and formless demon…" (227).

Aza's personality splits more completely than it ever has before. Despite the efforts of her rational self to prevent her, Aza gives into her anxious self's demand that she drink hand sanitizer. Note the use of capital letters to show how dominant the demon within her is. It seems to Aza that she has entirely lost the battle. She writes, "I wasn't possessed by a demon. I was the demon" (229). There no longer is a rational self fighting back: she drinks the hand sanitizer.

TWENTY

Questions:

41. What changes for Aza in this chapter?

Commentary:

The first significant change in this chapter is that Aza refers to herself in the second person (you) where previously she had done so almost always in the first person (I). This does not mean that she has lost touch with her own identity, for if that had happened the narrator would have referred to herself in the third person (she). Rather, the retrospective narrator is trying to get the reader to put him- herself in Aza's position. As we read, Aza includes us in her dilemma: instead of simply reading a description of what she went through, we go through it with her.

Aza has always told her mother that she is fine. Never before had she been honest as she is now when she barely squeezes out the words she needs to say, "'I'm in trouble, Mom. Big trouble" (231).' (This reminds me of Alcoholics Anonymous where the first step is to admit to being an alcoholic.)

TWENTY-ONE

Notes:

"catatonic" (236) – immobile both physically and psychologically.
"misogynistic" (240) – strongly prejudiced against women.
"Jane Austen" (240) – (1775-1817) English novelist – all of her six novels deal with courtship, love and marriage – but no sex!

Questions:

42. Comment on the function of the first three paragraphs of this chapter.

43. Aza says that she finds what Daisy says about turtles to be "something akin to a spiritual revelation" (245). What does she mean?

44. Explain how Aza's relationship with her mother has changed by the end of this chapter.

Commentary:

The chapter begins with what appears to be a 'happy ending': having "descended into proper madness" (note the narrator's deliberate use of an oxymoron), Aza begins "to make the connection that crack open the long-dormant case of Russell Pickett's disappearance" not in spite of but because of her "brain circuitry"; she learns "a way to live with the madness"; she becomes "a great detective"; and she walks off into the sunset with "Davis or Daisy" (232). This is how "proper" stories are supposed to end, but it is *not* how Aza's story ended. What does happen is that Dr. Singh gets a lot more assertive about Aza taking her medication and about her self-destructive behavior. She also changes her medication. None of that will solve Aza's problem because her problem cannot be solved; it can only be managed.

When she returns to school, Daisy is there for her, reassuring her that, for all the frustration of being friends with a crazy person, she still loves her. Daisy explains that Aza is not the "shit river" on which Indianapolis was built but the "okay city" that was built on an unpromising location. Recall that an earlier commentary noted that for Aza the unattainable perfect is the enemy of the good: that is precisely what Daisy is trying to tell her, "'You work with what you have'" (243). Daisy repeats the story about the earth resting on the backs of an infinite number of turtles and tells her, "'You're trying to find the turtle at the bottom of the pile, but that's not how it works'" which comes as "something akin to a spiritual revelation" to Aza (245). [Incidentally, Daisy's line, "'That reminds me of a story my mom tells'" (244) is a really unconvincing way to introduce the turtles story. Daisy's mother works in a dry cleaners' shop. How would she have come across this story and what possible interest would it have for her?]

Armed with a new confidence, Aza tells her mother about the $50,000 she got from Davis and insists that she intends to keep it. Finally, her mother agrees. Ms. Holmes has come to the point of admitting that Aza is not a child any more. She tells her, "'I keep saying I can't lose you, but I will. I am. And that's a hard thought … But you're right. You're not me. You make your own choices'" (247). Actually, the first choice Aza makes is to force Daisy and Mychal to talk to each other, which at least shows that she is thinking about other people.

TWENTY-TWO

Notes:

"*campylobacter*" (251) – campylobacteriosis, an infectious disease caused by bacteria – only life-threatening in very rare special cases.
"*Epstein-Barr*" (251) – human herpesvirus 4 is spread most commonly through bodily fluids, primarily saliva (e.g., through kissing or sharing drinks, food, or personal items, like toothbrushes) – symptoms are normally mild and temporary.
"dudebro" (253) – derogatory term for white suburban males, usually 16-25 years of age who are into 'guy-stuff.'
"Known City" (255) – Indianapolis has a lot of art collectives, but this one appear to be fictional.
"Pogue's Run tunnel" (255) – "Pogue's Run is real. It runs under Indianapolis for two-and-a-half miles, and it's possible to walk from one end to another" (atlasobscura.com).
"nucleotide mutation" (257) – "In biology, a mutation is the permanent alteration of the nucleotide sequence of the genome of an organism, virus, or extrachromosomal DNA or other genetic elements. Mutations result from errors during DNA replication or other types of damage to DNA…" (Wikipedia article, "Mutation").
"Herron" (258) – "[The] Herron School of Art and Design is the only accredited, professional art and design school in the state of Indiana" (Official Website).
"culvert" (259) – tunnel carrying an open stream, drain or sewer under a road or railway.

Questions:

45. Why does Aza break up with Davis? Or is it Davis who breaks up with Aza? Do you think this is the end of their Relationship with a capital R?

46. Explain what you think has happened to Russell Pickett.

Commentary:

Pogue's Run tunnel is certainly a unique place for an art exhibition (even an underground art exhibition). Since basically a sewer runs through it, one would think that, with her fear of bacteria, Aza would be totally incapable of entering the tunnel, but surprisingly it is Daisy who is unsure and Aza who reassures her, "'See, it's fine … [The rat] lives here … We're the invaders'" (260). It is Aza who proposes going for a walk "'down the tunnel,'" and who persuades Daisy to go with her (262). Aza uses the total darkness of the tunnel to illustrate to Daisy what her anxiety feels like, "'you're floating around in a body with no control. You don't get to decide … You're just stuck in there, totally alone in the darkness'" (263). Daisy begins to understand how bad it is for Aza.

For one of the first times in the story, Aza *is* able, for an extended time, to experience life in the moment without any intrusives. She and Daisy go "out to the meadow that night" talking about the things that teen girls talk about. Aza writes, "I didn't feel like I was watching a movie of our conversation. I was having it. I could listen to her, and I knew she was listening to me" (266). From the edge of the tunnel she sees Indianapolis as "blindingly bright … it took a minute before I remembered that this was nighttime, that this silver-lit landscape is what passed, aboveground, for darkness" (265). It is at this point, a point of 'normality,' not of 'craziness,' that Aza and Daisy begin to solve the mystery of Russell's disappearance. They have found themselves at the mouth of the White River in Pogue's Run and suddenly the line in Russell's post about "The jogger's mouth" (116) makes sense.

Once again, Green is careful to avoid sentimentality: finding the location of Russell's body does not change everything because it is not a first cause; it is not the one thing we know on which other knowledge can be built' it is not the answer to the question, 'On what does the last turtle stand?' because there is no last turtle. Aza explains, "The truth always disappoints … Nothing had been fixed, not really … You never find answers, just new and deeper questions" (267). What is remarkable, however, is how calmly Aza is able to accept this.

TWENTY-THREE

Questions:

47. How *should* this story end?

Commentary:

When Aza tells Davis about his father, for the first time in the narrative she is not the most vulnerable person in the room, and she has to support and comfort him. For once when she is hugging him she does not fall victim to intrusive thoughts about the danger of infection that she is running. It is Aza who takes the reasonable position, pointing out that Davis has seven years until his father is pronounced legally dead – seven years in which "to build a new life." She is, however, honest enough not to promise him that he can rely on her, "I wished I could tell him that he had me, that he could count on me, but he couldn't" (274).

Aza has realized that "'The problem with happy endings … is that they're either not really happy, or not really endings…'" The truth about "'real life [is] … some things get better and some things get worse. And then eventually you die'" (276). That is also the point of Davis's final blog, "nothing lasts" but why, he asks does he "have to miss everyone so much?" (277). Of course, there is no answer to that question. Life does not provide answers, only better questions.

TWENTY-FOUR

Questions:

48. From what point of view does Aza tell her story? How effective do you find this ending?

49. In the final paragraph, Aza writes, "But you don't know any of that yet. We squeeze his hand" (286). Comment on the use of pronouns in those two sentences.

Commentary:

Aza has been writing her narrative from the perspective of adulthood. It seems likely that she has written it at the suggestion of a psychiatrist who has told her, "*Write it down, how you got here*" (285). The lesson she has learned is life goes on, "And you go on, too, when the current is with you and when it isn't" (280). You cope with the harsh truth that "To live is to be missing": that is, you miss all those who were once in your life and are now, for whatever reason, gone (281). Aza knows now that the girl who lay looking at the night sky with Davis "would go on," although she certainly would not 'live happily ever after' (285).

The use of pronouns is important in this final chapter. Dr. Singh once told Aza, "'Self is a plurality, but pluralities can also be integrated, right? Think of a rainbow'" – to which Aza replied, "'Okay, well, I feel more like seven things than one thing'" (87). That is why in this chapter when describing herself as she was at sixteen, Aza uses the first person plural, "We squeeze his [Davis's] hand" (286). However, which she speaks of her adult self, she uses the first person singular, "I know a shrink would say" (285).

Notice that she also uses first person singular to describe her feelings as she looks up at the sky with him, because from Davis she has learned that "Spirals grow infinitely small the farther you follow them inward, but they also grow infinitely large the father you follow them out" (284). Finally, Aza does achieve the integration that Dr. Singh said was possible, because she learns to look up not down, outward not inward. She writes, "I, a singular pronoun, would go on, if always in a conditional tense" (285).

Perspectives

As always, Green's latest is moving and at times heartbreaking. His writing is beautiful and seamless. It's also funny, sharp and deeply relatable – even for a reader who's never experienced the kind of debilitating anxiety that affects Aza. Green brings her thoughts and fears to life just that vividly. (Chopin)

Green is rightfully praised for his dialogue, and the teen relationships in this book are convincing. But the inner monologues he writes for Aza are what truly stand out, as they paint the picture of her spiraling mind. (Chopin)

In 286 pages, "Turtles All the Way Down" simulates what it's like to participate in society while struggling with a mental disorder. In a society where mental illness is stigmatized, John Green gives a voice to those fighting with their minds. For anyone who has ever been trapped in their own thoughts and anxieties, and equally for those who have not, this book is a must-read. (Hardgrove)

[A] book some might find easy to not like. It is sentimental, occasionally clichéd and ticks so many teen fiction boxes you sometimes wonder if the author has a form beside him (troubled teen narrator – check; love interest – check; adults who don't understand – check; quirky best friend - check; scene where boy points out stars to girl – check; topical issue – check).(Haig)

This is by no means a perfect novel. The mystery and love story and mental health aspects often feel compartmentalised [*sic*] and it is 50 pages too long. Aza can be a repetitive narrator: this may be appropriate for someone who suffers repetitive thoughts, but can make the reading experience frustrating. (Haig)

The first few chapters … are a little crude, a little awkward and a little slow to get off the ground. (Senior)

I still wasn't prepared for the ending of this novel. It's so surprising and moving and true that I became completely unstrung, incapable of reading it to my husband without breaking down. One needn't be suffering like Aza to identify with it. One need only be human. (Senior)

The thin but neatly constructed plot feels a bit like an excuse for Green to flex his philosophical muscles; teenagers questioning the mysteries of consciousness can identify with Aza, while others might wish that something—anything—really happens. (Kirkus Review)

I felt his characters rise out of the pages to become their own complex, real-life people. Anyone who has enjoyed Green before will definitely find a new favorite here and even those who are on the fence about him may find new intricacies and nuance to his storytelling… (BookBrowse Review)

As to why I only give it a 4 out of 5 stars is because it's not realistic at all for a contemporary novel. Like the things they say is [*sic*] completely out of the world not like normal teenagers would think or say at all. Also I am not attached to the characters it's like I just enjoyed the book but didn't fell [*sic*] in love with it. (Drexel)

It was a very real and honest story, with an honest ending. (Allie)

Spread the news: John Green has officially broken free of the sappy, lovesick formula that plagued his first novels … Unlike Green's previous works, which all revolved around love stories, Davis and Aza's relationship is a subplot of the book. This is refreshing compared to *Looking for Alaska* and *Paper Towns*, which explored and exalted teenage boys as they relentlessly pined after girls. (maeve15)

Bibliography

Green, John. *Turtles All the Way Down.* New York: Dutton Books, 2017. Print.

Allie. *Turtles All the Way Down.* Reading Books in Cafes. 22 Oct. 2017. Web. 22 Nov 2017.

Chopin, Allison. "John Green's *Turtles All the Way Down*: A missing billionaire and a teen's anxious mind." *Daily News*: Entertainment. 18 Nov 2017. Web. 21 Nov 2017.

Drexel, Freya. "*Turtles All the Way Down* Review." Thoughts of a Peculiar. 5 Nov. 2017. Web. 22 Nov 2017.

Grady, Constance. "John Green's new book is not a quirky sad romance. It's an existential teenage scream." *Vox*. 11 Oct. 2017. Web. 21 Nov 2017.

Haig, Matt. "*Turtles All the Way Down* by John Green review – a new modern classic." *The Guardian*. theguardian.com. 10 Oct 2017. Web. 21 Nov 2017.

Hardgrove, Leah. "Real world OCD in John Green's *Turtles All the Way Down.*" *Student Life*. 9 Nov 20017. Web. 21 Nov 2017.

Kirkus Review. "*Turtles All the Way Down* by John Green." *Kirkus*. kirkusreview.com. 10 Oct 2017. Web. 21 Nov 2017.

Maeve15. "*Turtles All the Way Down* by John Green." *Teen Ink*. 27 Nov. 30. Web. Nov. 2017.

Menard, J. T. "Book Scene: *Turtles* dives into the mind of a teen with OCD." *Yakima Herald Republic*: Scene. 21 Nov. 2017. Web. 30 Nov 2017.

"Micro review: *Turtles All the Way Down.*" *The Times of India*: Life. 24 Nov. 2017. Web. 30 Nov. 2017.

Senior, Jennifer. "In John Green's *Turtles All the Way Down* A teenager's Mind Is at War With Itself." *The New York Times*, Books of *The Times*. 10 Oct 2017. Web. 21 Nov. 2017.

Szczechowski, Erin. Review: *Turtles All the Way Down* by John Green. *BookBrowse*. bookbrowse.com. 2017. Web. 22 Nov 2017.

"10 things to know about John Green's *Turtles All the Way Down.*"

Penguin UK. penguin.co.uk. 2017. Web. 21 Nov 2017.

"*Turtles All the Way Down.*" *Kenyon College*: Kenyon News. 30 June 2017. Web. 22 Nov. 2017.

Wikipedia contributors. *Turtles All the Way Down. Wikipedia, The Free Encyclopedia*. 20 Nov. 2017. Web. 22 Nov. 2017.

.

Literary terms activity

As you use each term in the study guide, fill in the definition of the term and include an example from the text to show how it is used. The first definition is supplied. Find an example in the text to complete it.

Term	Definition
	Example
Ambiguous, ambiguity	*When a statement is unclear in meaning- ambiguity may be deliberate or accidental*
Antagonist	
Climax	
Foreshadowing	
Hyperbole	
Image/imagery/ figurative language	

Term	Definition
	Example
Infer/inference	

Literary terms

Ambiguous, ambiguity: when a statement is unclear in meaning – ambiguity may be deliberate or accidental.

Analogy: a comparison which treats two things as identical in one or more specified ways.

Antagonist: a character or force opposing the protagonist.

Climax: the conflict to which the action has been building since the start of the play or story.

Colloquialism: the casual, informal mainly spoken language of ordinary people – often called "slang."

Comic hyperbole: deliberately inflated, extravagant language used for comic effect.

Connotation: the ideas, feelings and associations generated by a word or phrase.

Dark comedy: comedy which has a serious implication – comedy that deals with subjects not usually treated humorously (e.g., death).

Dialogue: a conversation between two or more people in direct speech.

Euphemism: a polite word for an ugly truth – for example, a person is said to be sleeping when they are actually dead.

Fallacy: a misconception resulting from incorrect reasoning.

First person: first person singular is "I" and plural is "we".

Foreshadow: a statement or action which gives the reader a hint of what is likely to happen later in the narrative.

Genre: the type of literature into which a particular text falls (e.g. drama, poetry, novel).

Hyperbole: exaggeration designed to create a particular effect.

Image, imagery: figurative language such as simile, metaphor, personification etc., or a description which conjures up a particularly vivid picture.

Imply, implication: when the text suggests to the reader a meaning which it does not actually state.

Infer, inference: the reader's act of going beyond what is stated in the text to draw conclusions.

Irony, ironic: a form of humor which undercuts the apparent meaning of a statement:

Conscious irony: irony used deliberately by a writer or character;

Unconscious irony: a statement or action which has significance for the reader of which the character is unaware;

Dramatic irony: when an action has an important significance that is obvious to the reader but not to one or more of the characters;

Tragic irony: when a character says (or does) something which will have a serious, even fatal, consequence for him/ her. The audience is aware of the error, but the character is not;

Verbal irony: the conscious use of particular words which are appropriate to what is being said.

Juxtaposition: literally putting two things side by side for purposes of comparison and/ or contrast.

Literal: the surface level of meaning that a statement has.

Melodramatic: action and/or dialogue that is inflated or extravagant – frequently used for comic effect.

Metaphor, metaphorical: the description of one thing by direct comparison with another (e.g. the coal-black night). Extended metaphor: a comparison which is developed at length.

Mood: the feelings and emotions contained in and/ or produced by a work of art (text, painting, music, etc.).

Motif: a frequently repeated idea, image or situation in a text.

Motivation: why a character acts as he/she does – in modern literature motivation is seen as psychological.

Narrator: the voice that the reader hears in the text – not to be confused with the author.

Oxymoron: the juxtaposition of two terms normally thought of as opposite (e.g. the silent scream).

Paradox, paradoxical: a statement or situation which appears self-contradictory and therefore absurd.

Perspective: point of view from which a story, or an incident within a story, is told.

Personified, personification: a simile or metaphor in which an inanimate object or abstract idea is described by comparison with a human.

Plot: a chain of events linked by cause and effect.

Protagonist: the character who initiates the action and is most likely to have the sympathy of the audience.

Pun: a deliberate play on words where a particular word has two or more meanings both appropriate in some way to what is being said.

Realism: a text that describes the action in a way that appears to reflect life.

Sarcasm: stronger than irony – it involves a deliberate attack on a person or idea with the intention of mocking.

Setting: the environment in which the narrative (or part of the narrative) takes place.

Simile: a description of one thing by explicit comparison with another (e.g. my love is like a red, red rose). Extended simile: a comparison which is developed at length.

Style: the way in which a writer chooses to express him/ herself. Style is a vital aspect of meaning since how something is expressed can crucially affect what is being written or spoken.

Suspense: the building of tension in the reader.

Symbol, symbolic, symbolism, symbolize: a physical object which comes to represent an abstract idea (e.g. the sun may symbolize life).

Themes: important concepts, beliefs and ideas explored and presented in a text.

Third person: third person singular is "he/ she/ it" and plural is "they" – authors often write novels in the third person.

Tone: literally the sound of a text – How words sound (either in the mouth of an actor or the head of a reader) can crucially affect meaning/

Vocabulary

How do we learn new words?

In the first four years of your life you learned more words than you will learn in the rest of your life! You did this by listening to other people speak. Simply by hearing a word over and over again, you worked out what it meant. (That's why most babies say the words 'mommy' or 'daddy' first.)

As we get older, we still use this method to learn new words, but it doesn't work so well. That is because the words that we still do not know tend not to come up too often, so we don't get that repetition that helps us to work out what the words mean. (How many times are you likely to come across the word 'opaque' in the next month? It is in this novel, but you are unlikely to hear or read it again for a while!)

As a result, we have to make a deliberate effort to learn new words. Here is the best way:

1. When you first see the word, try to relate it to other words that you already know. For example, 'mysticism' sounds like 'mystery' which means 'a puzzle, something unusual which does not have an obvious solution.'
2. Look at the word in context. If you are able to relate it to a word that you know, does this meaning make any sense? Does the context add to your understanding of what the new word means? If you are unable to relate the word to one that you already knew, try reading the sentence with a blank where the new word goes. Ask yourself what word or phrase would you put into the blank to make sense in this context. Put your thoughts and guesses on the first line.
3. Check the dictionary definition of the word. Remember that every word has a range of meanings. You need to know what the word means in the context in which it is used.

Vocabulary: Chapters One to Nine

1. cacophony, noun (3): discordant, harsh noise.

2. parasitic, adj. (3): living on something else and taking nourishment from it (like a bloodsucker).

3. irrational, adj. (3): founded on emotion rather than reason; illogical; senseless.

4. contracted, verb (4): reduced, diminished in size.

5. unprecedented, adj. (4)

____

6. futile, adj. (6)

____

7. culmination, noun (14)

____

8. circumscribes, verb (16)

____

9. ushered, verb (29

____

10. pedantic, adj. (44)

____

11. intrigued, verb (54)

____

12. disembodied, adj. (54)

____

13. sentient, adj. (66)

____

14. hypothetically, adv. (77)

____

15. ostracize, verb (89)

____

16. exemplify, verb (89)

____

17. suffused, verb (99)

____

Vocabulary: Chapters Ten to Twenty-four

1. incongruous, adj. (119): out of place with its surroundings, inappropriate, strange.

2. meticulously, adv. (138): thoroughly, precisely, with attention to the smallest detail.

3. regaled, verb (138): entertained, delighted, amused people with talk.

4. regaled, verb (164): delegate, pass onto or down to another.

5. paranoid, adj. (191)

____

6. discernible, adj. (191)

____

7. lacerated, verb (222)

____

8. opaque, adj. (231)

____

9. ineffable, adj. (231)

____

10. inherently, adv. (232)

____

11. excruciatingly, adv. (233)

____

12. omnipresent, adj. (234)

____

13. exonerated, verb (255)

____

14. obligated, verb (256)

____

15. procrastinating verb (270)

____

Turtles All the Way Down by John Green

Vocabulary Test: Chapters One to Nine

Below are some sentences. Select the word from the vocabulary list that fits into each sentence: Select the word from the vocabulary list that fits into each sentence:

cacophony	parasitic	irrational	contracted	unprecedented
futile	culmination	circumscribes	ushered	pedantic
intrigued	disembodied	sentient	ostracize	exemplify
suffused	hypothetically			

a) Entering the narrow cave, my ________________ fear of the dark overcame me.

b) The crowd's reaction to the last-minute goal led to a ________________ of sound that filled the stadium.

c) The critic's hostile review of the production of *Hamlet* caused the theater management to ________________ him from future productions.

d) The trainer's attempts to treat the injury proved ________________ and the player went off.

e) Bringing out the family photograph album always ________________ in an evening of stories about 'the good old days.'

f) The car maker recalled ten thousand vehicles when it was discovered that, ________________, under certain circumstances, the air bags might not work.

g) The bank robbery was the ________________ of many months of planning and preparation.

h) The coach stressed that the team needed to make a/an ________________ effort to get back in the game.

i) Elaine focused on revising for her exclusion of her health, and as a result, she ________________ the flu and made herself ill.

j) These two individuals ________________ the radically different views that exist on the topic.

k) I was ________________ to find that the note contained no signature, just the initial J.

l) The sunset ________________ the western sky with shades of red.

m) All living, ______________ beings are formed out of atoms which are not themselves living.

n) When it came to MLA formatting, our teacher was ________________ and would mark in red the smallest error.

o) The Five Minutes Hate was announced by a ________________ voice that came through the loudspeakers.

p) I reject the idea that my biology entirely ________________ my identity leaving me without freedom.

q) In the trenches of World War One, almost every soldier suffered from ________________ infections like lice.

Vocabulary Test: Chapters Ten to Twenty-four

Below are some sentences. Select the word from the vocabulary list that fits into each sentence: Select the word from the vocabulary list that fits into each sentence:

incongruous	meticulously	regaled	devolved	paranoid
discernible	lacerated	opaque	ineffable	inherently
omnipresent	exonerated	obligated	excruciatingly	procrastinating

a) The detective examined the crime scene ________________ for evidence.

b) DNA evidence ________________ the man who had been convicted on the testimony of five eye witnesses.

c) When the actor playing Ophelia fell ill, responsibility for this crucial role ________________ naturally onto her understudy.

d) Despite a battery of tests, the doctor found no ________________ improvement in her patient..

e) After Thanksgiving dinner, grandpa ________________ the family with stories about 'the good old days.'

f) I keep meaning to go to the course "How to Stop ________________," but somehow I never get around to it!

g) Mountain climbing is ________________ risky but practice, the right equipment and caution can minimize the danger.

h) Removing an infected tooth would be ________________ painful were it not for anesthetic.

i) I mean, not to be ________________ or anything, but they are all out to get me.

j) The dilapidated, abandoned cottage looked ________________ between the two high-rise condominiums.

k) I felt __________________ to repay the $20 I had borrowed because I knew my friend needed the money.

l) The victim sustained a severely __________________ arm as he tried to fend off the knife attack.

m) Christianity conceives of God as perfect, omnipotent, and ___________________.

n) The medieval windows of the Saxon church were small, thick and largely _______________.

o) Aza cannot make sense of the ___________________ mystery of her own identity.

A Controversial Text:

John Green writes, "I've received more than ten thousand emails in the last six years from teenagers, and zero of them – actually and literally zero – have expressed any kind of concern or discomfort with the so-called 'mature content' of my books" ("And Now a Word," *An Abundance of John* Greens).

Research specific cases of objections to his novels being used in schools and/or made available in libraries. For each case identify and assess the objections and explain the decisions made. Where you agree, do not be afraid to say so. For example, I would personally object to this book being used in a Middle School!

You should also read Sherman Alexie's reply to criticism of his novel *The Absolutely True Diary of a Part-Time Indian* in his article, "Why the Best Kids Books Are Written in Blood" (*The Wall Street Journal*, June 9, 2011). It is easy to find on the Internet. Here is perhaps his most powerful statement: "Almost every day, my mailbox is filled with handwritten letters from students – teens and pre-teens – who have read my YA book and loved it. I have yet to receive a letter from a child somehow debilitated by the domestic violence, drug abuse, racism, poverty, sexuality, and murder contained in my book." There is plenty of material here for discussion.

1. Which of these views most closely reflects your own?

a. Every parent must approve of a book before it is placed on a school reading list.
b. Every parent must approve of a book before it is required reading.
c. Every parent must approve of a book before it is taught in class.
d. Parents of individual students may opt out of reading any prescribed book; an acceptable alternative will be provided.
e. Schools should be sensitive to parental views but ultimately schools set required reading.
f. A book should only be dropped if a majority of parents object to it.

If I have not even come close to stating your own view, formulate it yourself. Now argue it out in groups.

2. In groups, make a list of your ten favorite books – books that you think *every* young person should read. Now work out how many of them would get through a. above. Just to help you out, here are some really popular books that parents often seek to get banned: *Macbeth*, *Huck Finn*, *Tom Sawyer*, *To Kill a Mockingbird*, *Catcher in the Rye*, *Catch-22*, and *Beloved*. Were any of these on your group top-ten?

3. Research your own favorite book. Has it ever been banned anywhere? Has any individual or group ever *tried* to get it banned? Why?

4. Of course, we all support the First Amendment, and we obviously want parents to be actively involved in their children's schools, but what do we do when parents want to ban books? How much say, if any, should the kids who are going to read the book have?

5. Write a letter either advocating or objecting to the banning of *Paper Towns* in schools. You need to be quite specific about your objections to / defense of the novel including examples and quotations. There is only one tiny catch: you have to take the side in this debate which is the *opposite* of what you actually believe.

6. As an alternative to #5, hold a mock School Board meeting in your classroom. With a vote at the end!

Appendix 1: Reading Group Use of the Study Guide Questions

Although there are both closed and open questions in the Study Guide, very few of them have simple, right or wrong answers. They are designed to encourage in-depth discussion, disagreement, and (eventually) consensus. Above all, they aim to encourage readers to go to the text to support their conclusions and interpretations.

I am not so arrogant as to presume to tell readers how they should use this resource. I used it in the following ways, each of which ensured that group members were well prepared for group discussion and presentations.

1. Set a reading assignment for the group and tell everyone to be aware that the questions will be the focus of whole group discussion at the next meeting.

2. Set a reading assignment for the group and allocate particular questions to sections of the group (e.g. if there are four questions, divide the group into four sections, etc.).

In the meeting, form discussion groups containing one person who has prepared each question and allow time for feedback within the groups.

Have feedback to the whole the on each question by picking a group at random to present their answers and to follow up with a group discussion.

3. Set a reading assignment for the group, but do not allocate questions.

In the meeting, divide readers into groups and allocate to each group one of the questions related to the reading assignment, the answer to which they will have to present formally to the meeting.

Allow time for discussion and preparation.

4. Set a reading assignment for the group, but do not allocate questions.

In the meeting, divide readers into groups and allocate to each group one of the questions related to the reading assignment.

Allow time for discussion and preparation.

Now reconfigure the groups so that each group contains at least one person who has prepared each question and allow time for feedback within the groups.

5. Before starting to read the text, allocate specific questions to individuals or pairs. (It is best not to allocate all questions to allow for other approaches and variety. One in three questions or one in four seems about right.) Tell readers that they will be leading the group discussion on their question. They will need to start with a brief presentation of the issues and then conduct a question and answer session. After this, they will be expected to present a brief review of the discussion.

6. Having finished the text, arrange the meeting into groups of 3, 4 or 5. Tell each group to select as many questions from the Study Guide as there are members of the group.

Each individual is responsible for drafting out an answer to one question, and each answer should be substantial.

Each group as a whole is then responsible for discussing, editing and suggesting improvements to each answer.

Appendix 2: Vocabulary Test Answers

Chapters One to Nine

Select the word from the vocabulary list that fits into each sentence:

cacophony	parasitic	irrational	contracted	unprecedented
futile	culmination	circumscribe	sushered	pedantic
intrigued	disembodied	sentient	ostracize	exemplify
suffused	hypothetically			

a) Entering the narrow cave, my **irrational** fear of the dark overcame me.

b) The crowd's reaction to the last-minute goal led to a **cacophony** of sound that filled the stadium.

c) The critic's hostile review of the production of *Hamlet* caused the theater management to **ostracize** him from future productions.

d) The trainer's attempts to treat the injury proved **futile** and the player went off.

e) Bringing out the family photograph album always **ushered** in an evening of stories about 'the good old days.'

f) The car maker recalled ten thousand vehicles when it was discovered that, **hypothetically**, under certain circumstances, the air bags might not work.

g) The bank robbery was the **culmination** of many months of planning and preparation.

h) The coach stressed that the team needed to make an **unprecedented** effort to get back in the game.

i) Elaine focused on revising for her exclusion of her health, and as a result, she **contracted** the flu and made herself ill.

j) These two individuals **exemplify** the radically different views that exist on the topic.

k) I was **intrigued** to find that the note contained no signature, just the initial J.

l) The sunset **suffused** the western sky with shades of red.

m) All living, **sentient** beings are formed out of atoms which are not themselves living.

n) When it came to MLA formatting, our teacher was **pedantic** and would mark in red the smallest error.

o) The Five Minutes Hate was announced by a **disembodied** voice that came through the loudspeakers.

p) I reject the idea that my biology entirely **circumscribes** my identity leaving me without freedom.

q) In the trenches of World War One, almost every soldier suffered from **parasitic** infections like lice.

Turtles All the Way Down by John Green

Vocabulary Test Answers: Chapters Ten to Twenty-Four

Select the word from the vocabulary list that fits into each sentence:

incongruous	meticulously	regaled	devolved	paranoid
discernible	lacerated	opaque	ineffable	inherently
omnipresent	exonerated	obligated	excruciatingly	procrastinating

a) The detective examined the crime scene **meticulously** for evidence.

b) DNA evidence **exonerated** the man who had been convicted on the testimony of five eye witnesses.

c) When the actor playing Ophelia fell ill, responsibility for this crucial role **devolved** naturally onto her understudy.

d) Despite a battery of tests, the doctor found no **discernible** improvement in her patient..

e) After Thanksgiving dinner, grandpa **regaled** the family with stories about 'the good old days.'

f) I keep meaning to go to the course "How to Stop **Procrastinating**," but somehow I never get around to it!

g) Mountain climbing is **inherently** risky but practice, the right equipment and caution can minimize the danger.

h) Removing an infected tooth would be **excruciatingly** painful were it not for anesthetic.

i) I mean, not to be **paranoid** or anything, but they are all out to get me.

j) The dilapidated, abandoned cottage looked **incongruous** between the two high-rise condominiums.

k) I felt **obligated** to repay the $20 I had borrowed because I knew my friend needed the money.

l) The victim sustained a severely **lacerated** arm as he tried to fend off the knife attack.

m) Christianity conceives of God as perfect, omnipotent, and **omnipresent**.

n) The medieval windows of the Saxon church were small, thick and largely **opaque.**

o) Aza cannot make sense of the **ineffable** mystery of her own identity.

Appendix 3: Plot graph

Plot graph for *Turtles All The Way Down*

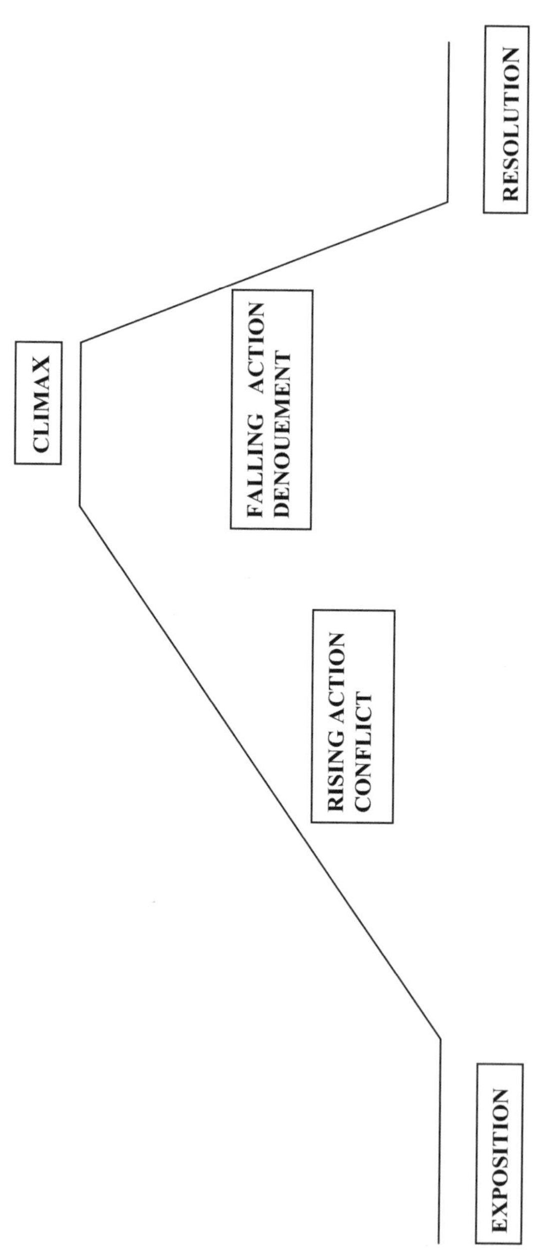

Appendix 4: Body outline: Female

Body Outline: Male

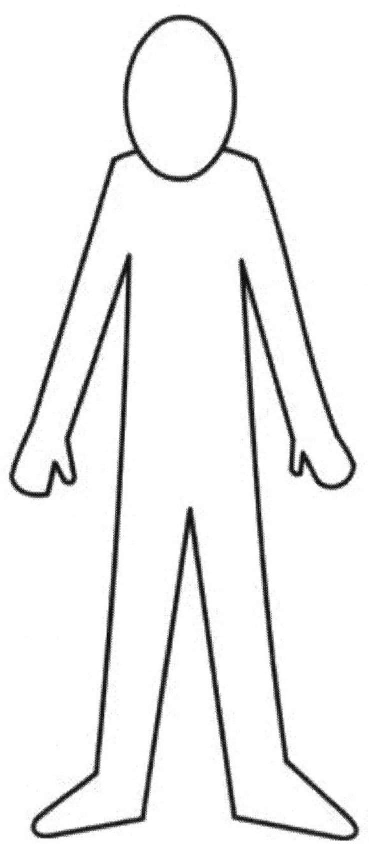

To the Reader,

Ray Moore was born in Nottingham, England. He obtained his Master's Degree in Literature from Lancaster University and taught in secondary education for twenty-eight years before relocating to Florida with his wife. There he taught English and Information Technology in the International Baccalaureate Program at Vanguard High School in Ocala. He is now a full-time writer and fitness fanatic.

Website: http://www.raymooreauthor.com

Ray strives to make his texts the best that they can be. If you have any comments or question about this book *please* contact the author through his email: villageswriter@gmail.com

Also by Ray Moore:

All books are available from amazon.com and from barnesandnoble.com as paperbacks and at most online eBook retailers.

Fiction:

The Lyle Thorne Mysteries: each book features five tales from the Golden Age of Detection:

Investigations of The Reverend Lyle Thorne
Further Investigations of The Reverend Lyle Thorne
Early Investigations of Lyle Thorne
Sanditon Investigations of The Reverend Lyle Thorne
Final Investigations of The Reverend Lyle Thorne
Lost Investigations of The Reverend Lyle Thorne
Official Investigations of Lyle Thorne

Non-fiction:

The *Critical Introduction series* is written for high school teachers and students and for college undergraduates. Each volume gives an in-depth analysis of a key text:

"The General Prologue" by Geoffrey Chaucer: A Critical Introduction
"The Great Gatsby" by F. Scott Fitzgerald: A Critical Introduction
"Pride and Prejudice" by Jane Austen: A Critical Introduction
"The Stranger" by Albert Camus: A Critical Introduction (Revised Second Edition)

The *Text and Critical Introduction series* differs from the Critical introduction series as these books contain the original text and in the case of the medieval texts an interlinear translation to aid the understanding of the text. The commentary allows the reader to develop a deeper understanding of the text and themes within the text.

"Sir Gawain and the Green Knight": Text and Critical Introduction

"The General Prologue" by Geoffrey Chaucer: Text and Critical Introduction

"Heart of Darkness" by Joseph Conrad: Text and Critical Introduction

"Henry V" by William Shakespeare: Text and Critical Introduction

"Oedipus Rex" by Sophocles: Text and Critical Introduction

"A Room with a View" By E.M. Forster: Text and Critical Introduction

"The Sign of Four" by Sir Arthur Conan Doyle Text and Critical Introduction

"The Wife of Bath's Prologue and Tale" by Geoffrey Chaucer: Text and Critical Introduction

Study guides available in print - listed alphabetically by author

* denotes also available as an eBook

"ME and EARL and the Dying GIRL" by Jesse Andrews: A Study Guide

"Pride and Prejudice" by Jane Austen: A Study Guide

"Moloka'i" by Alan Brennert: A Study Guide

"Wuthering Heights" by Emily Brontë: A Study Guide *

"Jane Eyre" by Charlotte Brontë: A Study Guide *

"The Stranger" by Albert Camus: A Study Guide

"The Myth of Sisyphus" and "The Stranger" by Albert Camus: Two Study Guides *

Study guide to "Death Comes to the Archbishop" by Willa Cather

"The Awakening" by Kate Chopin: A Study Guide

Study Guide to Seven Short Stories by Kate Chopin

Study Guide to "Ready Player One" by Ernest Cline

Study Guide to "Disgrace" by J. M. Coetzee

"The Meursault Investigation" by Kamel Daoud: A Study Guide

*Study Guide on "Great Expectations" by Charles Dickens**

"The Sign of Four" by Sir Arthur Conan Doyle: A Study Guide *

"The Wasteland, Prufrock and Poems" by T.S. Eliot: A Study Guide

Study Guide on "Birdsong" by Sebastian Faulks

"The Great Gatsby" by F. Scott Fitzgerald: A Study Guide

"A Room with a View" by E. M. Forster: A Study Guide

"Looking for Alaska" by John Green: A Study Guide

"Paper Towns" by John Green: A Study Guide

"Catch-22" by Joseph Heller: A Study Guide *

Turtles All the Way Down by John Green

"Unbroken" by Laura Hillenbrand: A Study Guide
"The Kite Runner" by Khaled Hosseini: A Study Guide
"A Thousand Splendid Suns" by Khaled Hosseini: A Study Guide
"The Secret Life of Bees" by Sue Monk Kidd: A Study Guide
Study Guide on "The Invention of Wings" by Sue Monk Kidd
"Go Set a Watchman" by Harper Lee: A Study Guide
"On the Road" by Jack Keruoac: A Study Guide
*"Life of Pi" by Yann Martel: A Study Guide **
Study Guide to "The Bluest Eye" by Toni Morrison
"Animal Farm" by George Orwell: A Study Guide
Study Guide on "Nineteen Eighty-Four" by George Orwell
*Study Guide to "Selected Poems" and Additional Poems by Sylvia Plath**
"An Inspector Calls" by J.B. Priestley: A Study Guide
Study Guide on "Cross Creek" by Marjorie Kinnan Rawlings
"Esperanza Rising" by Pam Munoz Ryan: A Study Guide
"The Catcher in the Rye" by J.D. Salinger: A Study Guide
"Where'd You Go, Bernadette" by Maria Semple: A Study Guide
"Henry V" by William Shakespeare: A Study Guide
*Study Guide on "Macbeth" by William Shakespeare **
*"Othello" by William Shakespeare: A Study Guide **
"Oedipus Rex" by Sophocles: A Study Guide
"Cannery Row" by John Steinbeck: A Study Guide
"East of Eden" by John Steinbeck: A Study Guide
"The Grapes of Wrath" by John Steinbeck: A Study Guide
*"Of Mice and Men" by John Steinbeck: A Study Guide**
*"Antigone" by Sophocles: A Study Guide **
"Oedipus Rex" by Sophocles: A Study Guide
"The Goldfinch" by Donna Tartt: A Study Guide
"Walden; or, Life in the Woods" by Henry David Thoreau: A Study Guide
Study Guide to "Cat's Cradle" by Kurt Vonnegut
*"The Bridge of San Luis Rey" by Thornton Wilder: A Study Guide **
Study Guide on "The Book Thief" by Markus Zusak

Study Guides available as e-books:

A Study Guide on "Heart of Darkness" by Joseph Conrad
A Study Guide on "The Mill on the Floss" by George Eliot
A Study Guide on "Lord of the Flies" by William Golding
A Study Guide on "Nineteen Eighty-Four" by George Orwell

A Study Guide on "Henry IV Part 2" by William Shakespeare
A Study Guide on "Julius Caesar" by William Shakespeare
A Study Guide on "The Pearl" by John Steinbeck
A Study Guide on "Slaughterhouse-Five" by Kurt Vonnegut

New titles are added regularly.

Teacher resources:

Ray also publishes many more study guides and other resources for classroom use on the 'Teachers Pay Teachers' website: http://www.teacherspayteachers.com/Store/Raymond-Moore

Made in the USA
Columbia, SC
14 July 2019